AF448336

The fascination of the digital becomes artistic experience with John Drooyan. Because he is able to tell the human life and generally the cosmos with the power of a real artist. His colours, lines and themes are full of expressive power and they present themselves to the viewer by opening a window in a newer artistic world. "Digital Art" is John Drooyan's book! The book where the modern meets the widest public possible so to explain the treasures from a new adventure, from a challenge against the modern techniques and against the mysteries of the calculators which John Drooyan has won.

Il fascino del digitale diviene esperienza artistica con John Drooyan. Difatti è capace di raccontare la vita umana e in generale l'universo con la forza di un vero artista. I suoi colori, linee e temi sono pieni di potere espressivo e presentano loro stessi allo spettatore aprendo una finestra in un mondo artistico recente. "Digital Art" (Arte Digitale) è il libro di John Drooyan! Il libro dove il moderno incontra il più vasto pubblico possibile per spiegare i tesori provenienti da una nuova avventura, da una sfida alle nuove tecnologie e ai misteri dei computer, vinta da John Drooyan.

Dino Marasà

John Drooyan

285 West 6th St. #329,
San Pedro, California USA 90731
Tel. (310) 309-9430
E-mail: jdvisart@yahoo.com

on cover:
Babylon - "Headquarters" series, print on canvas, 84,5x69,2 cm (framed)

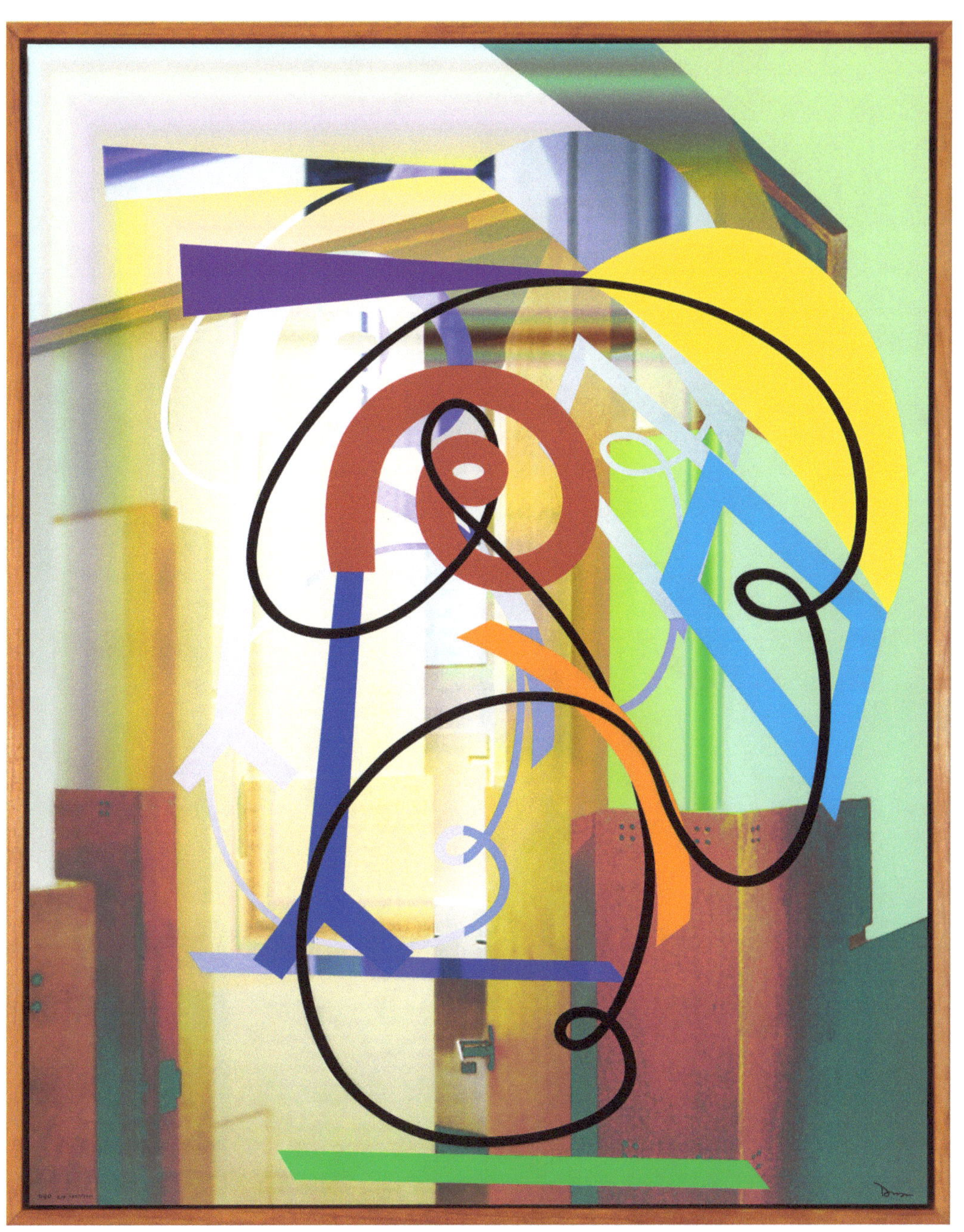

Ugo - "Headquarters" series, print on canvas, 87,3x67,3 cm (framed)

Digital Art - John Drooyan

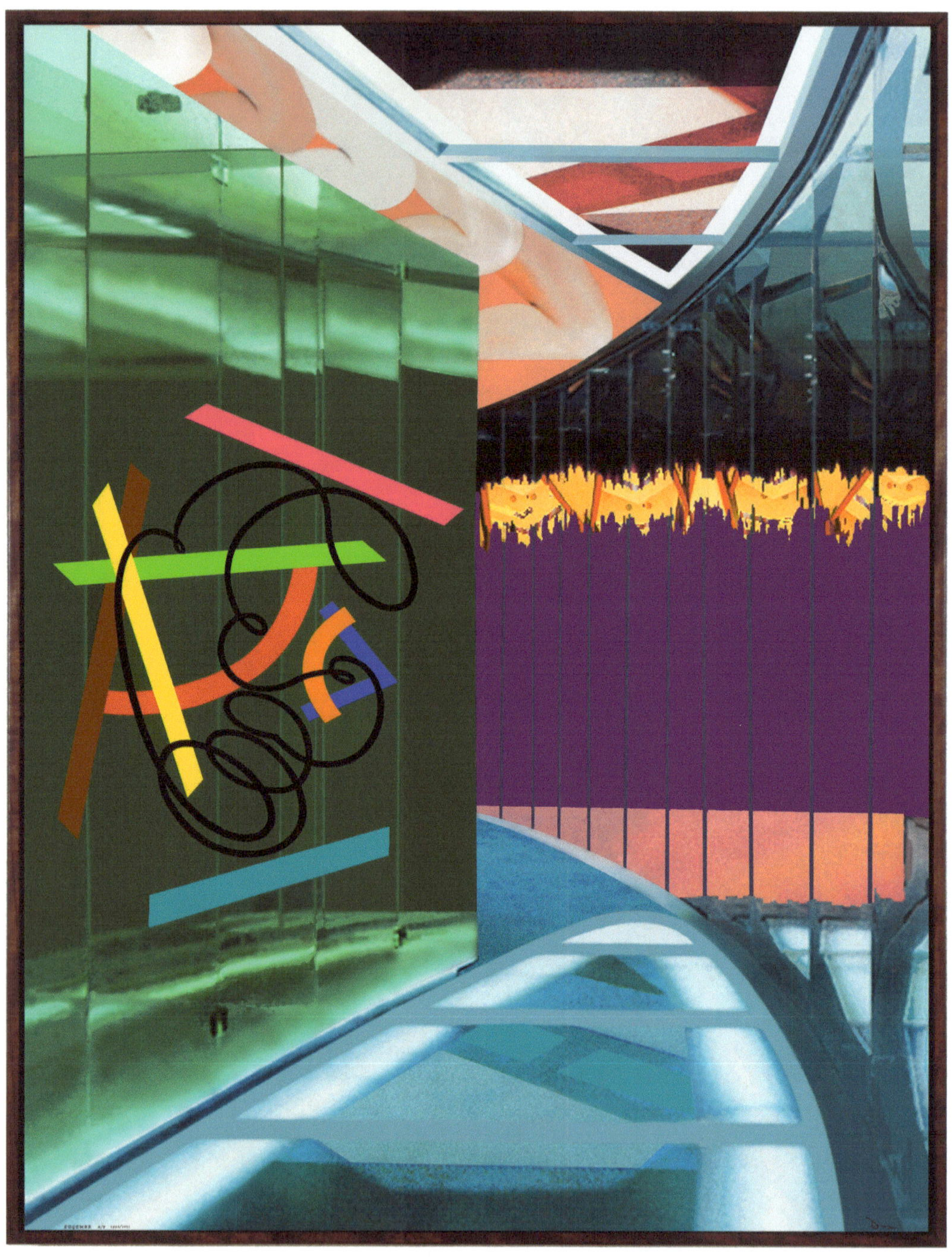

Edgemar - "Headquarters" series, print on canvas, 120,6x90 cm (framed)

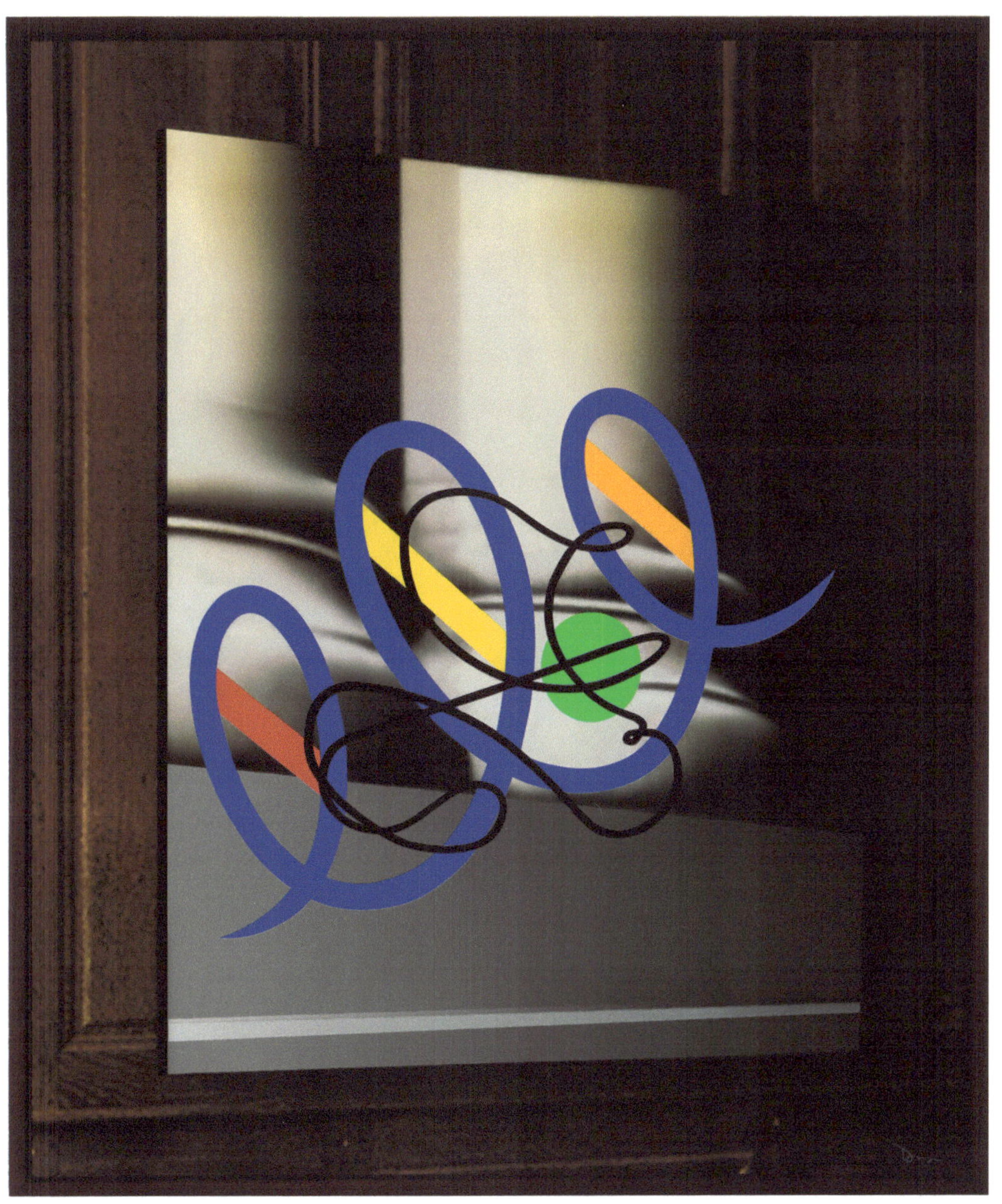

Babylon - "Headquarters" series, print on canvas, 84,5x69,2 cm (framed)

Digital Art - John Drooyan

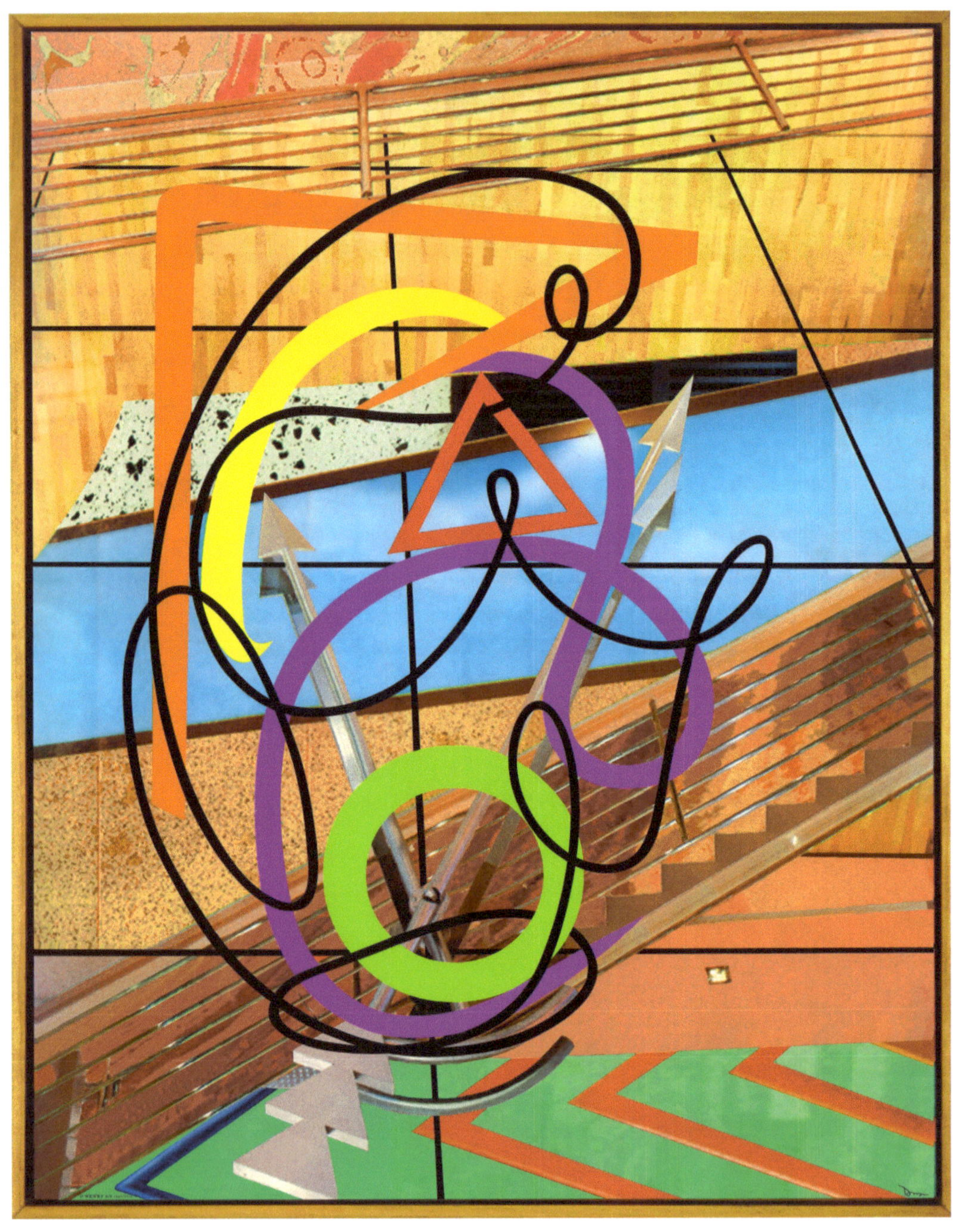

O' Henry - "Headquarters" series, print on canvas, 104.1x 79.7 cm (framed)

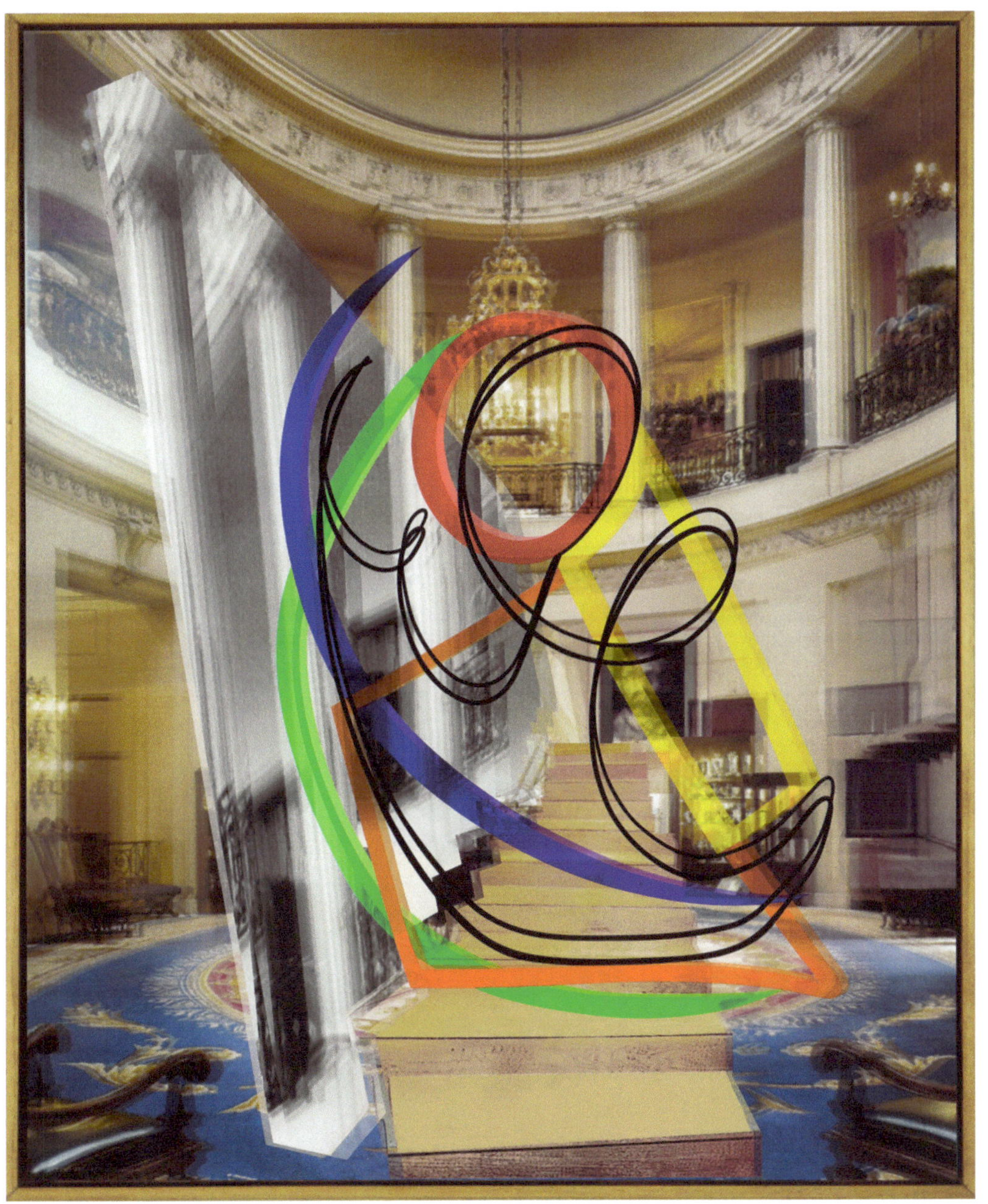

Status Anxiety - "Headquarters" series, print on canvas, 105.4x 84.5 cm (framed)

Digital Art - John Drooyan

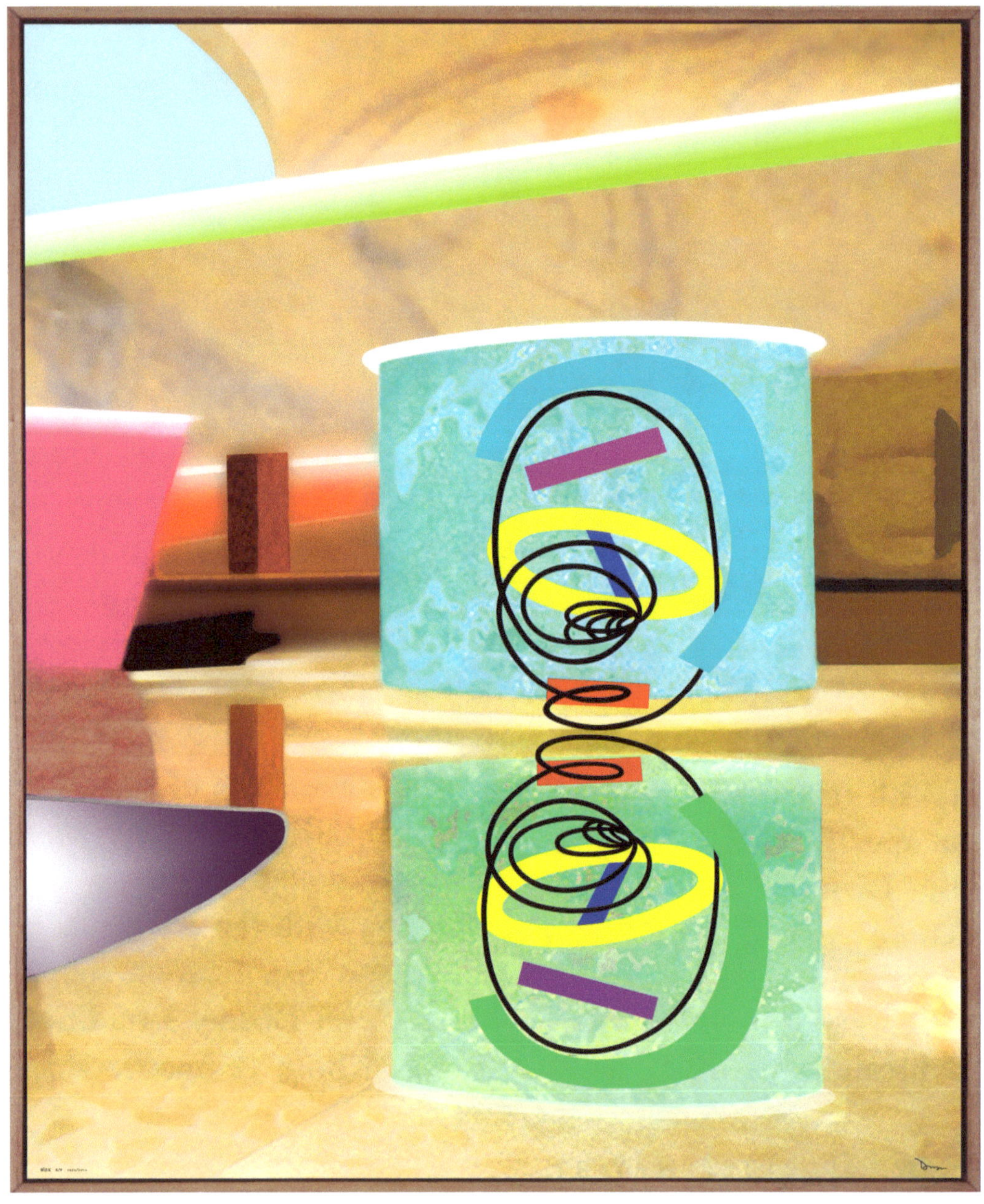

HOX - "Headquarters" series, print on canvas, 115.6x93.35 cm (framed)

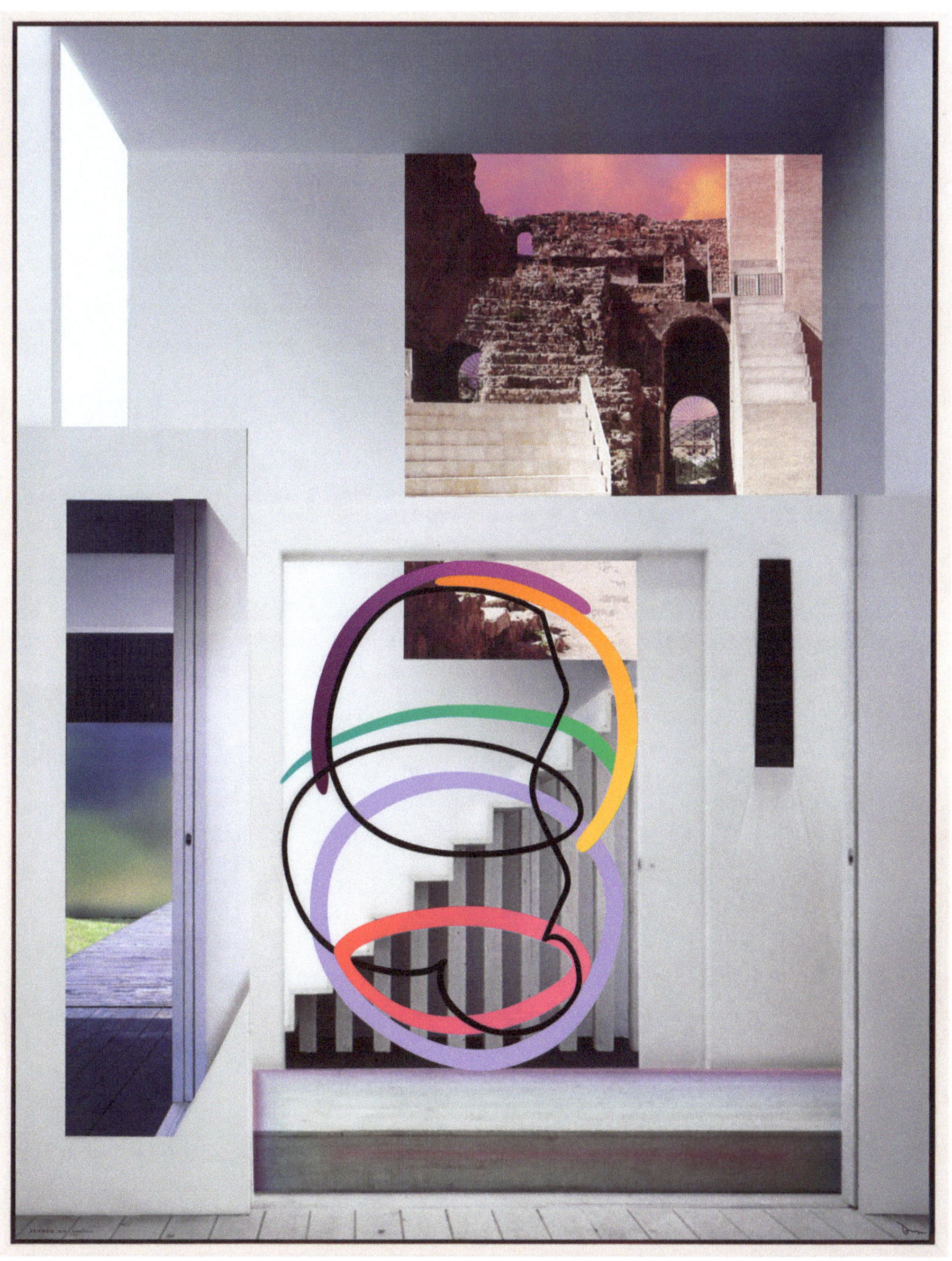

Xanadu - "Headquarters" series, print on canvas, 114.9x87.3 cm (framed)

Digital Art - John Drooyan

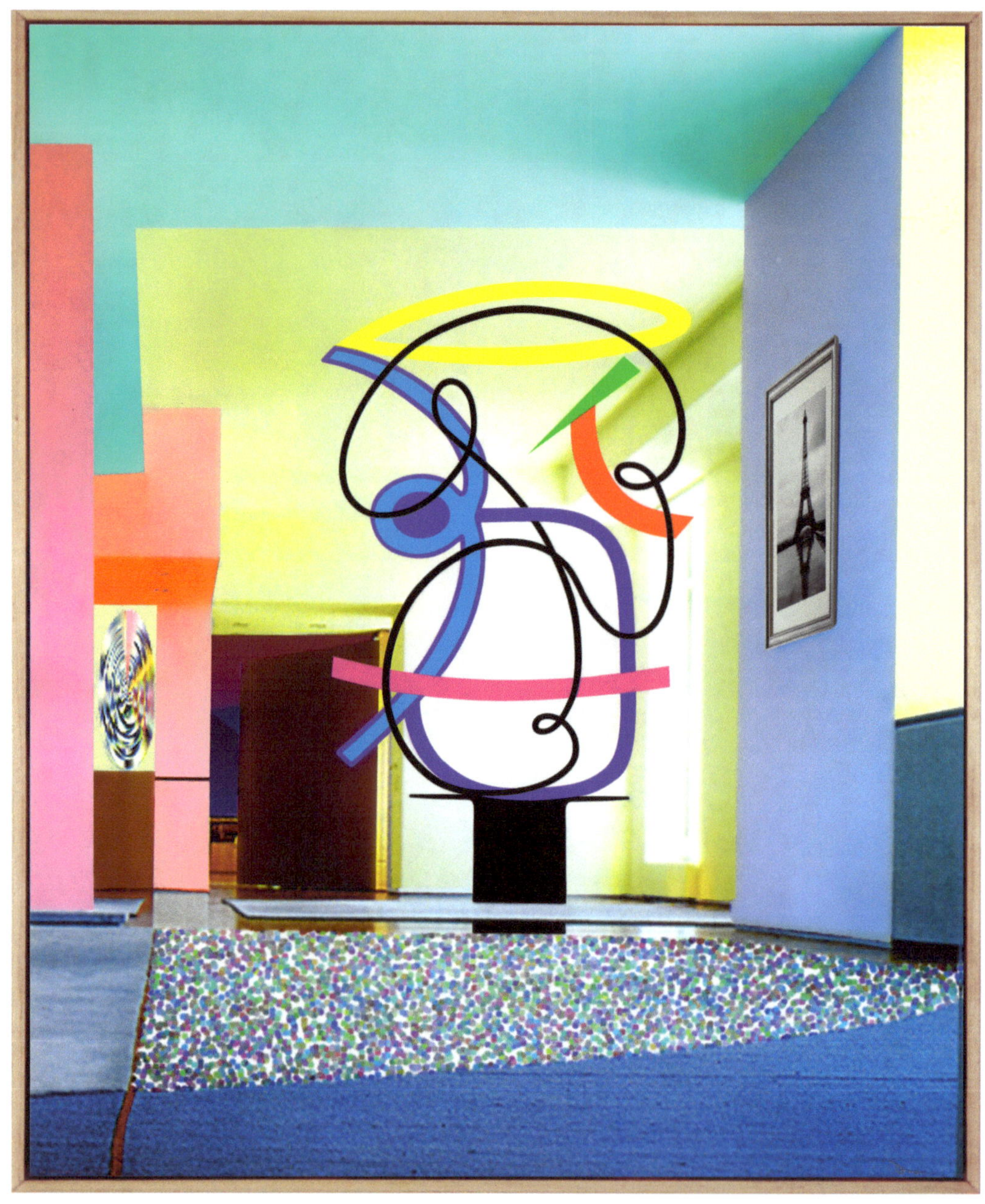

Le Chateau - "Headquarters" series, print on canvas, 109.9x88.9 cm (framed)

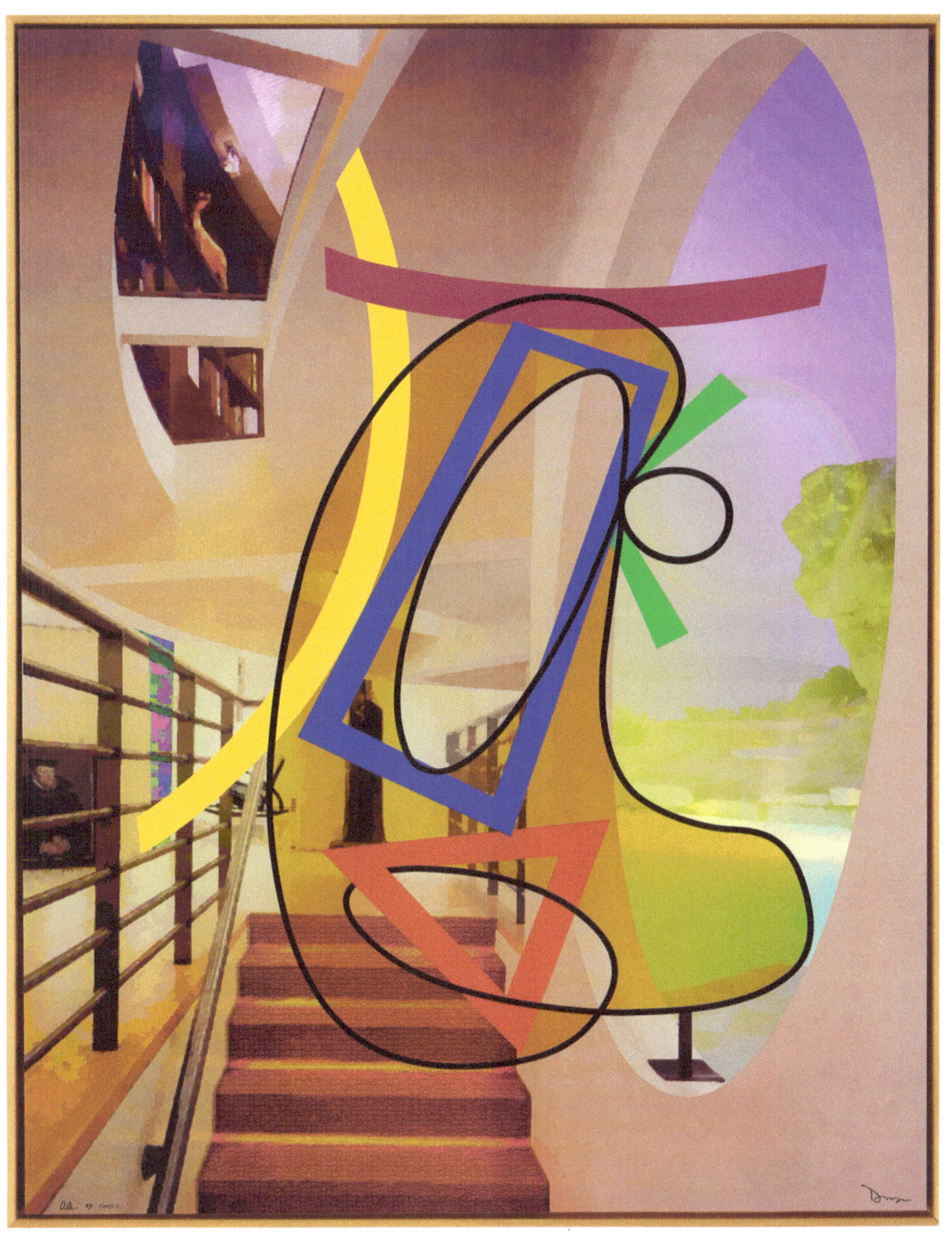

Olè - "Headquarters" series, print on canvas, 104.8x78.7 cm (framed)

Digital Art - John Drooyan

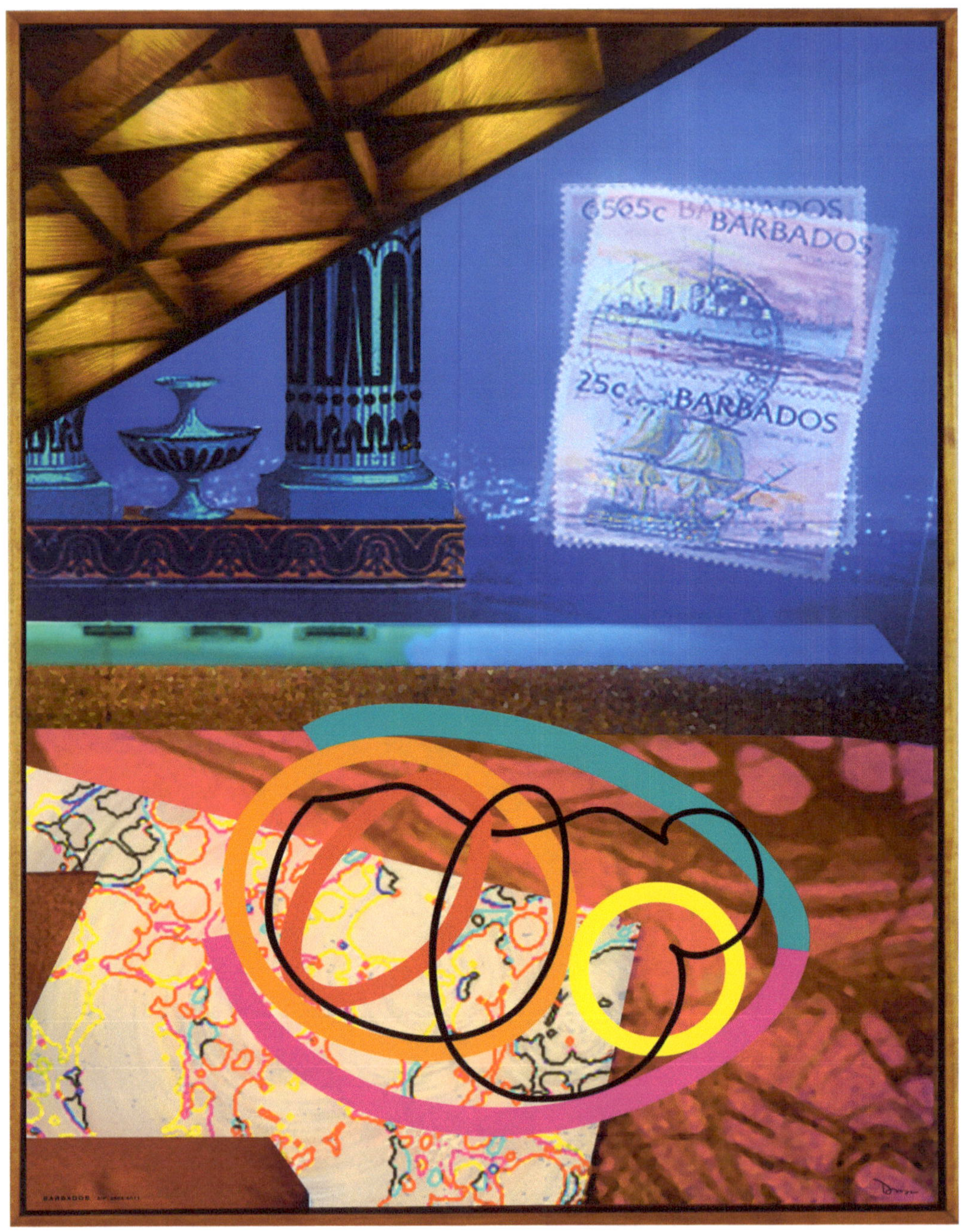

Barbados - "Headquarters" series, print on canvas, 105.9x81.3 cm (framed)

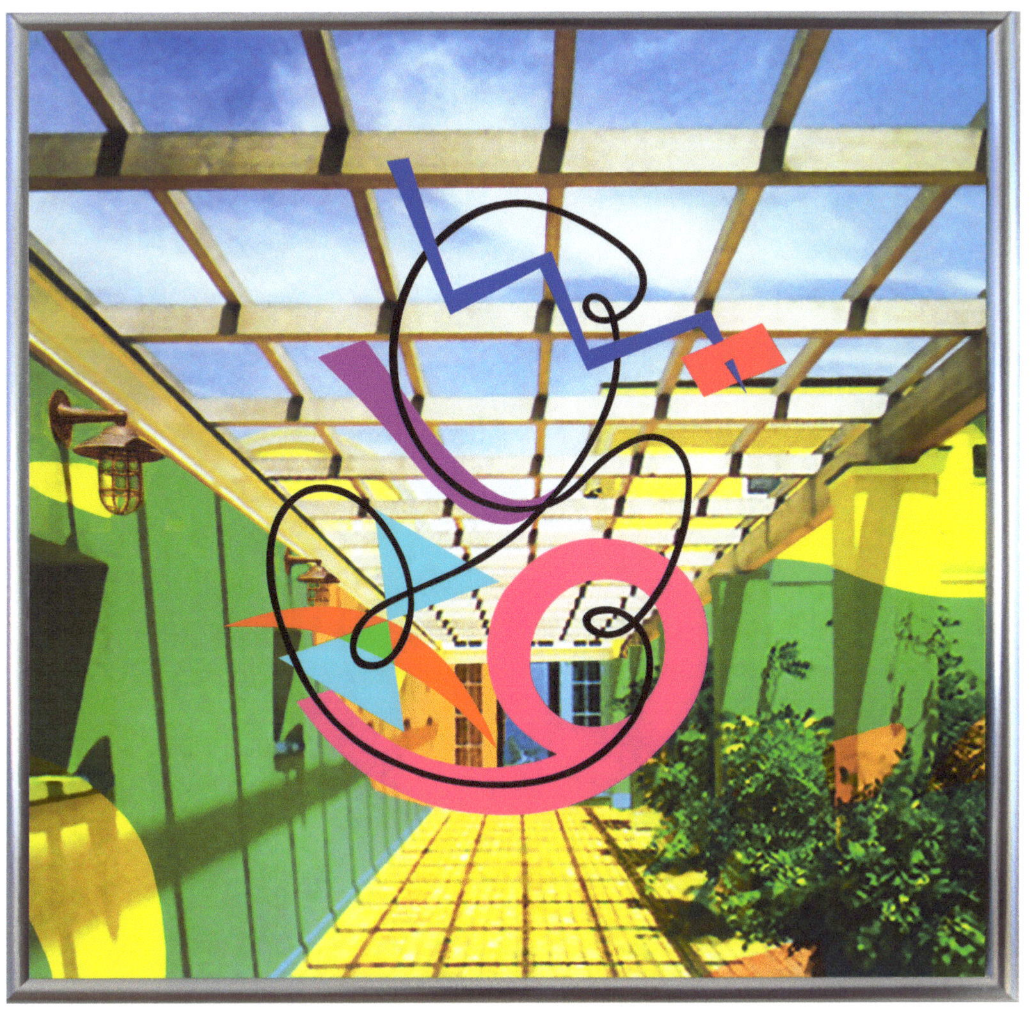

Baselville no. 1 - "Headquarters" series, print on canvas, 80x80 cm (framed)

Digital Art - John Drooyan

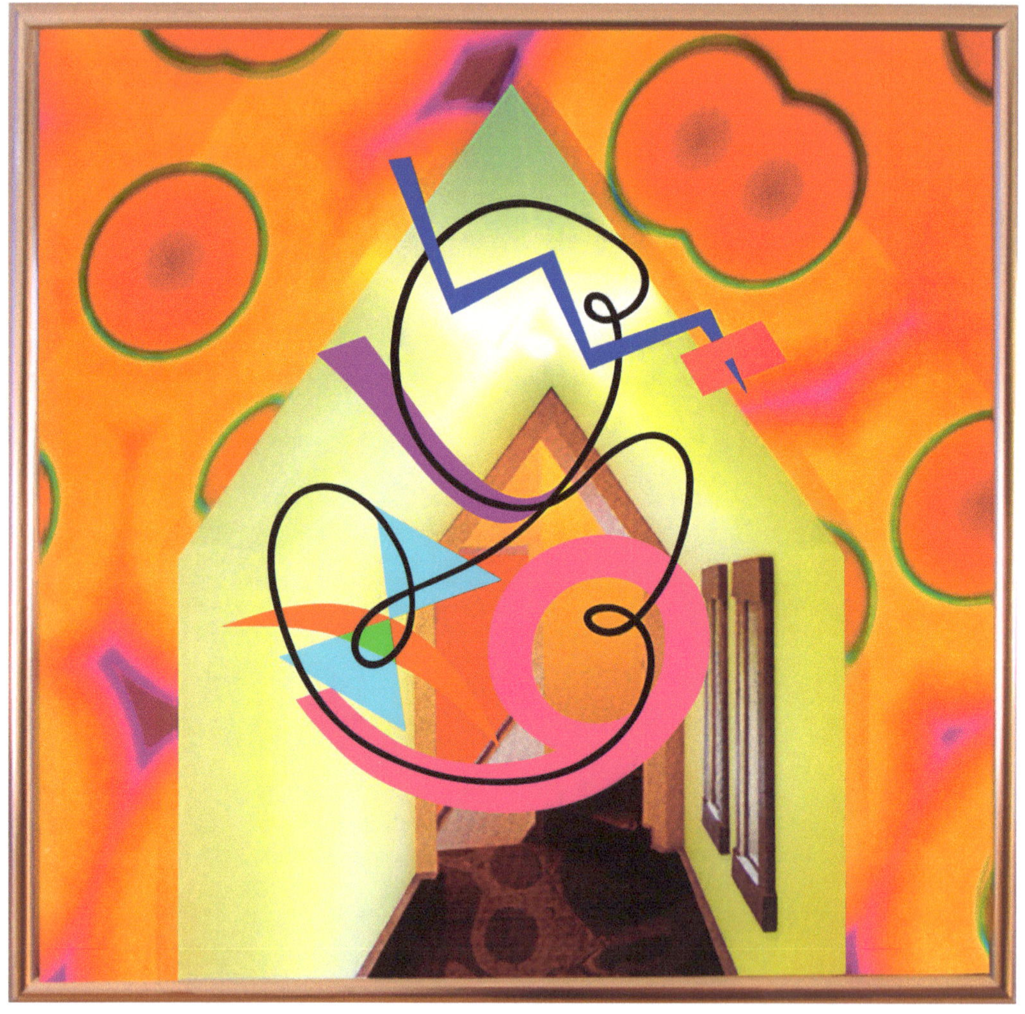

Baselville no. 2 - "Headquarters" series, print on canvas, 80x80 cm (framed)

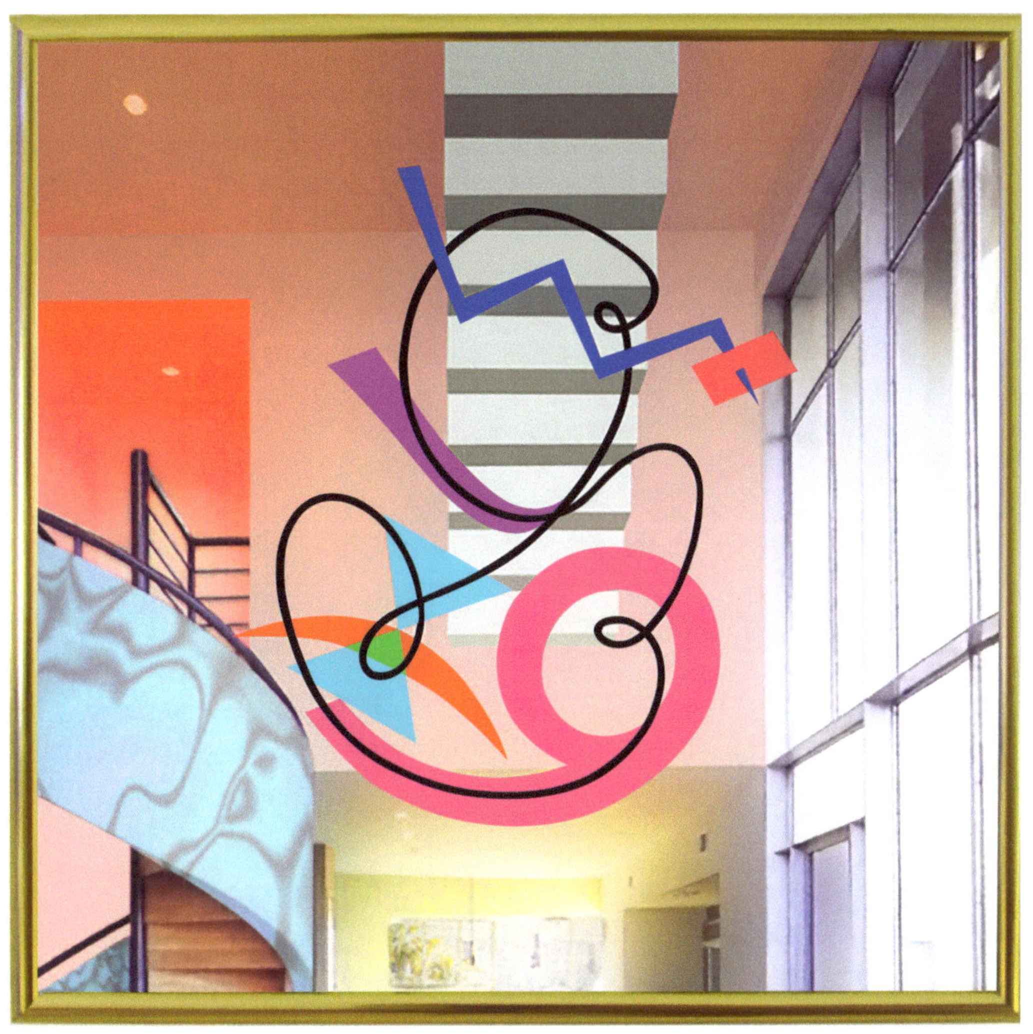

Baselville no. 3 - "Headquarters" series, print on canvas, 80x80 cm (framed)

Digital Art - John Drooyan

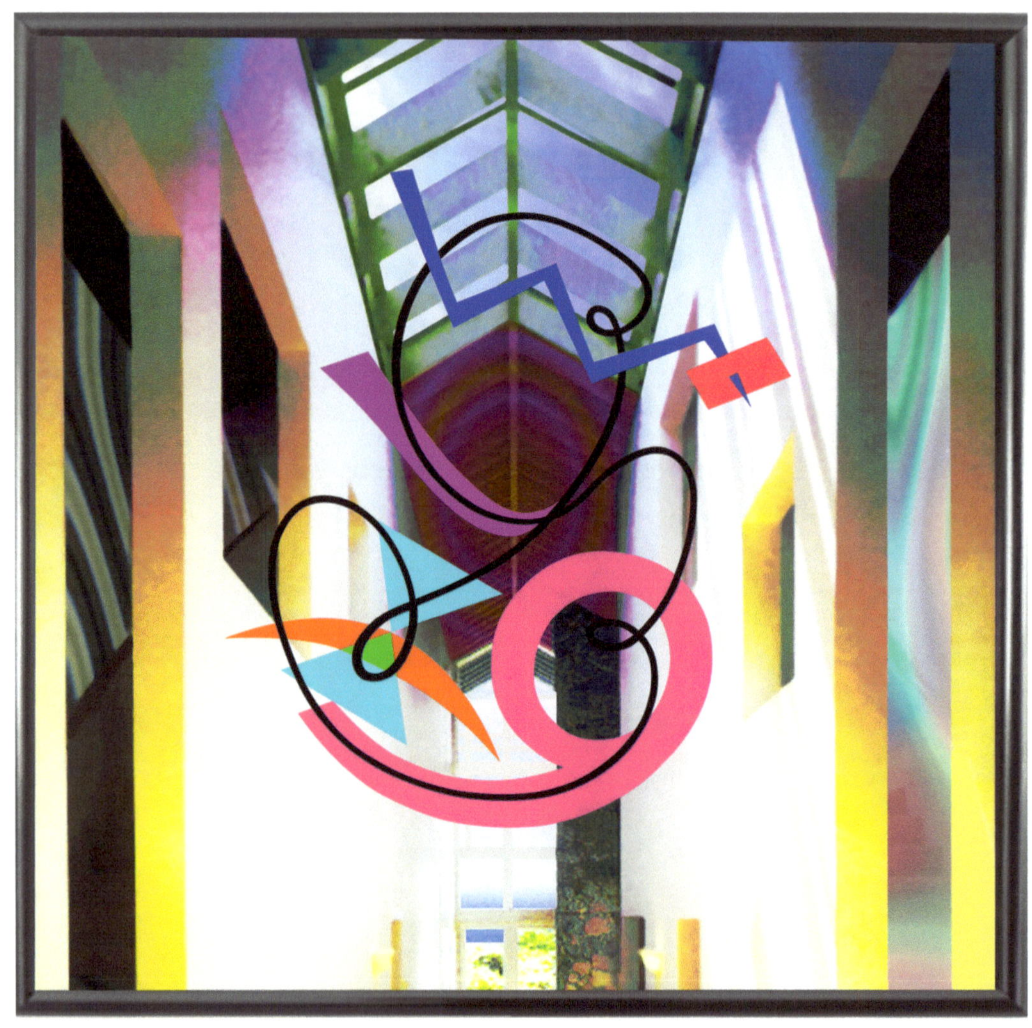

Baselville no. 4 - "Headquarters" series, print on canvas, 80x80 cm (framed)

Digital Art - **John Drooyan**

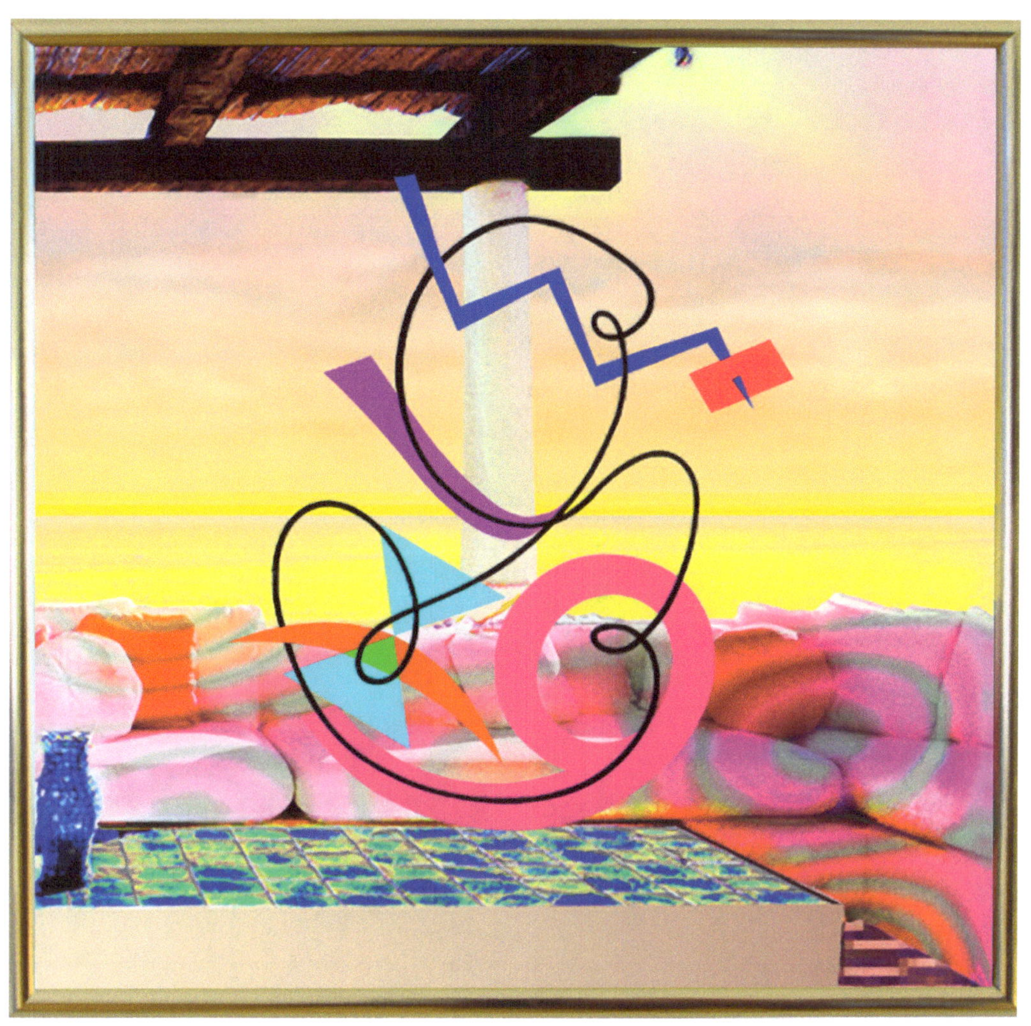

Baselville no. 5 - "Headquarters" series, print on canvas, 80x80 cm (framed)

Digital Art - John Drooyan

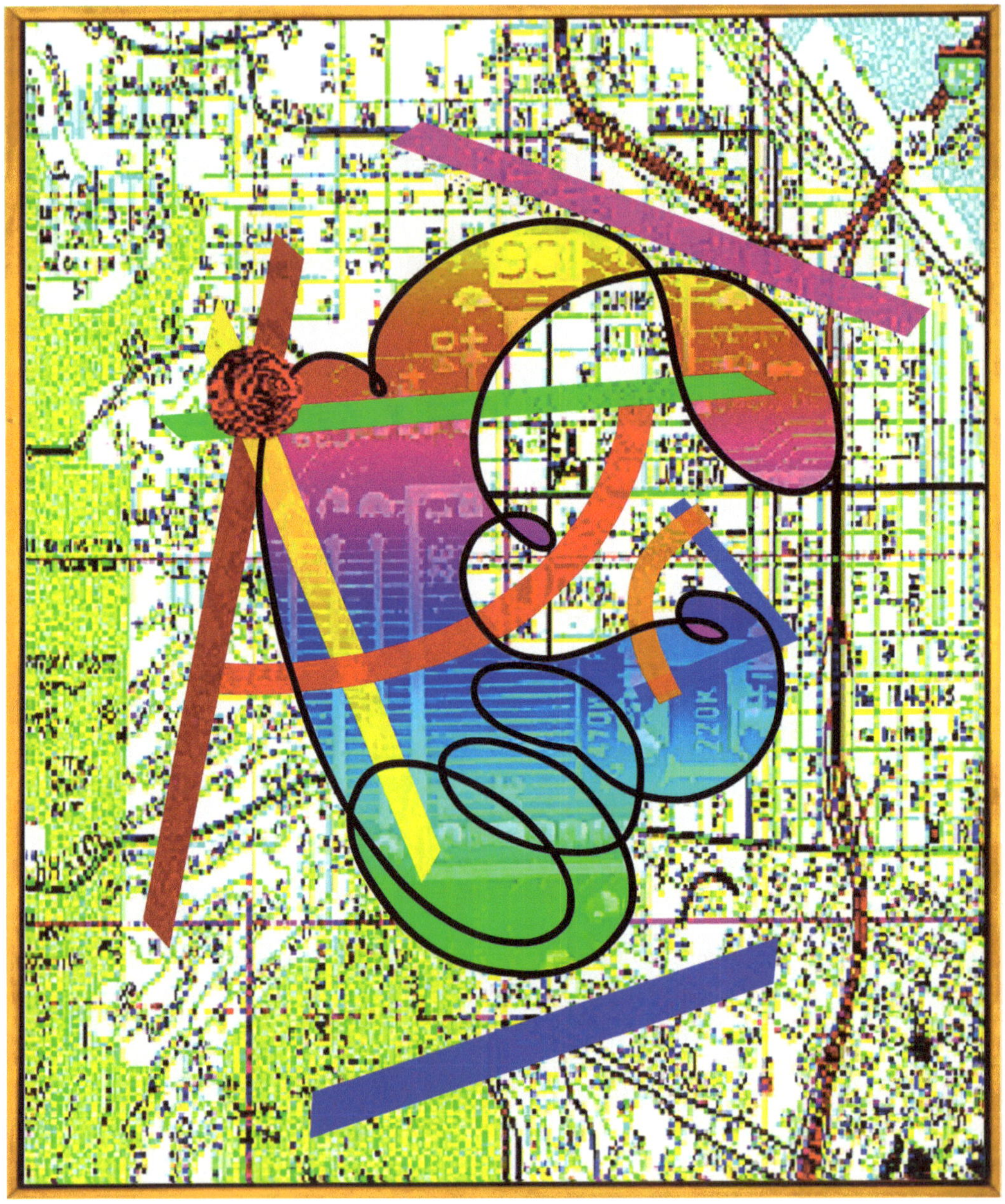

Emax - "Headquarters" series, print on canvas, 85.7x69.2 cm (framed)

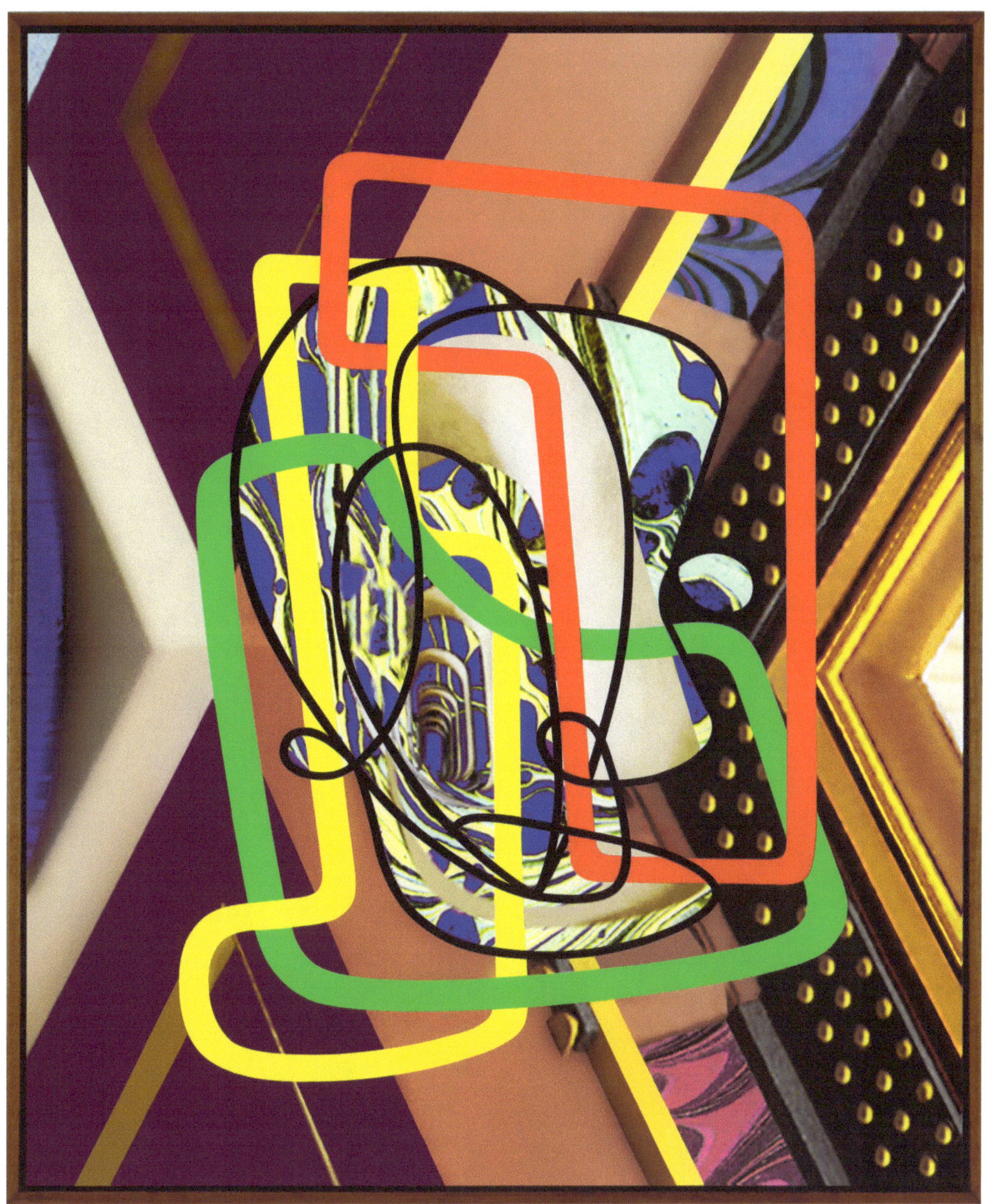

CEO - "Headquarters" series, print on canvas, 85.7x69.2 cm (framed)

Digital Art - John Drooyan

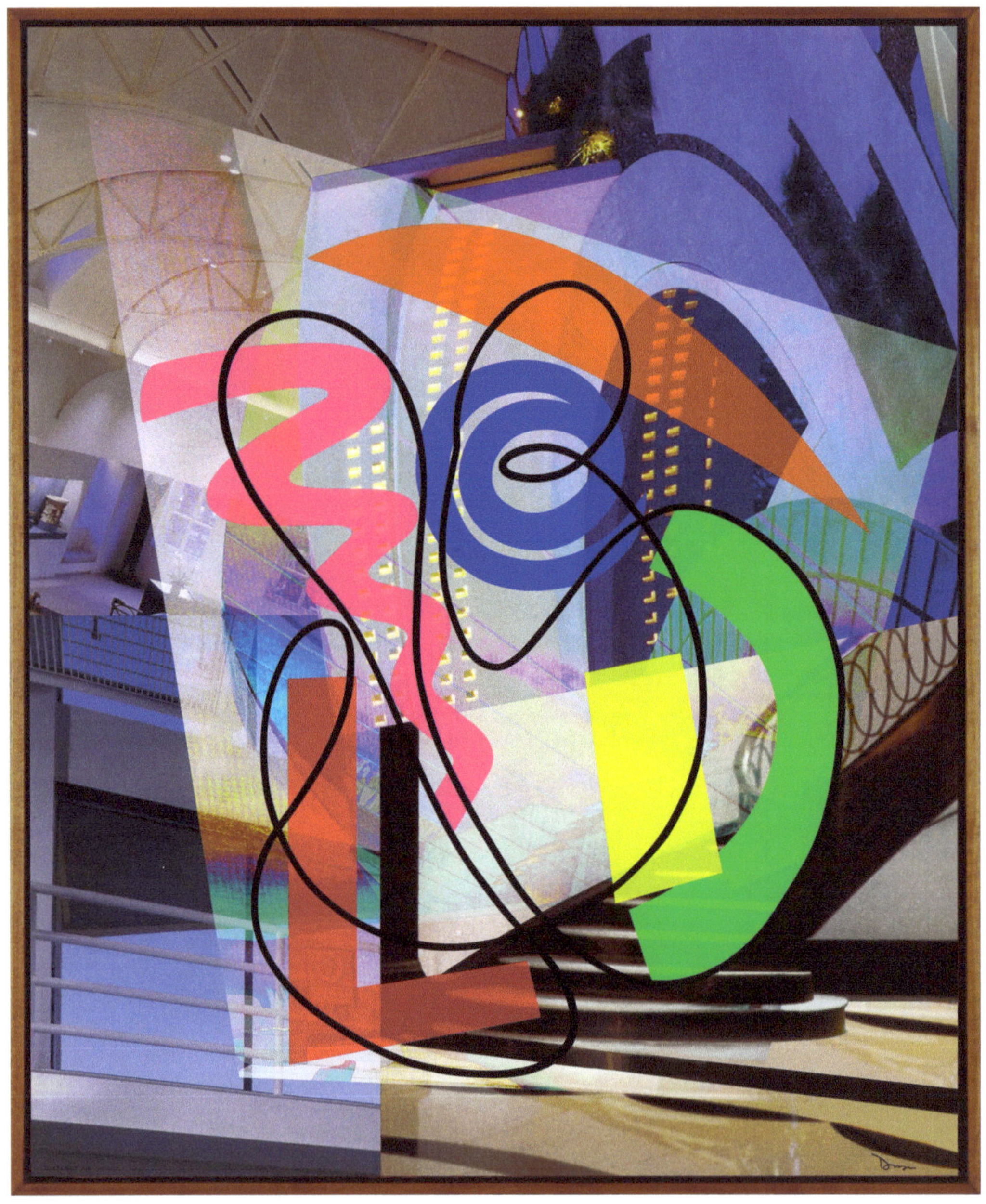

Class Act - "Headquarters" series, print on canvas, 85.7x69.2 cm (framed)

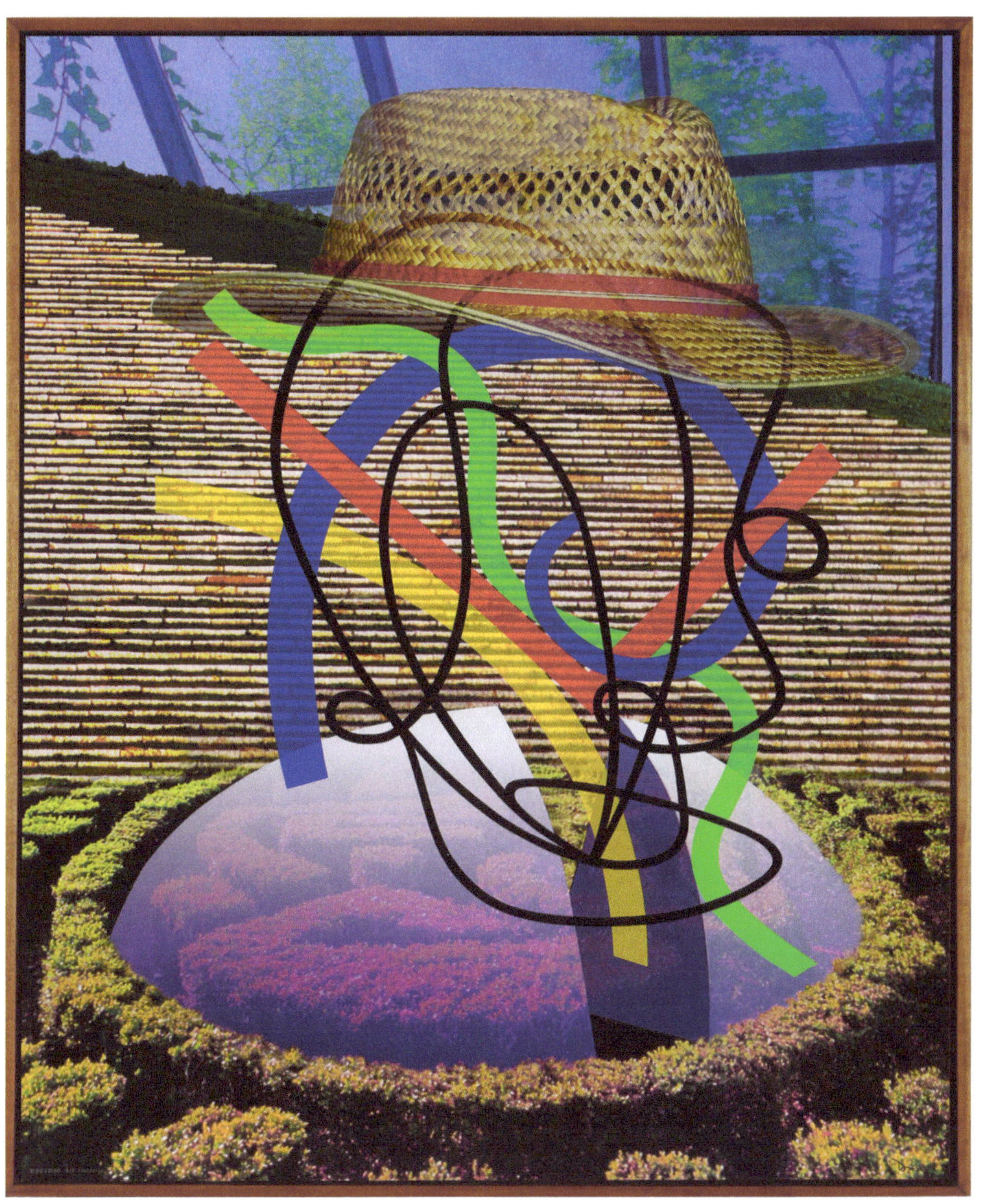

Decidio - "Headquarters" series, print on canvas, 85.7x69.2 cm (framed)

Digital Art - John Drooyan

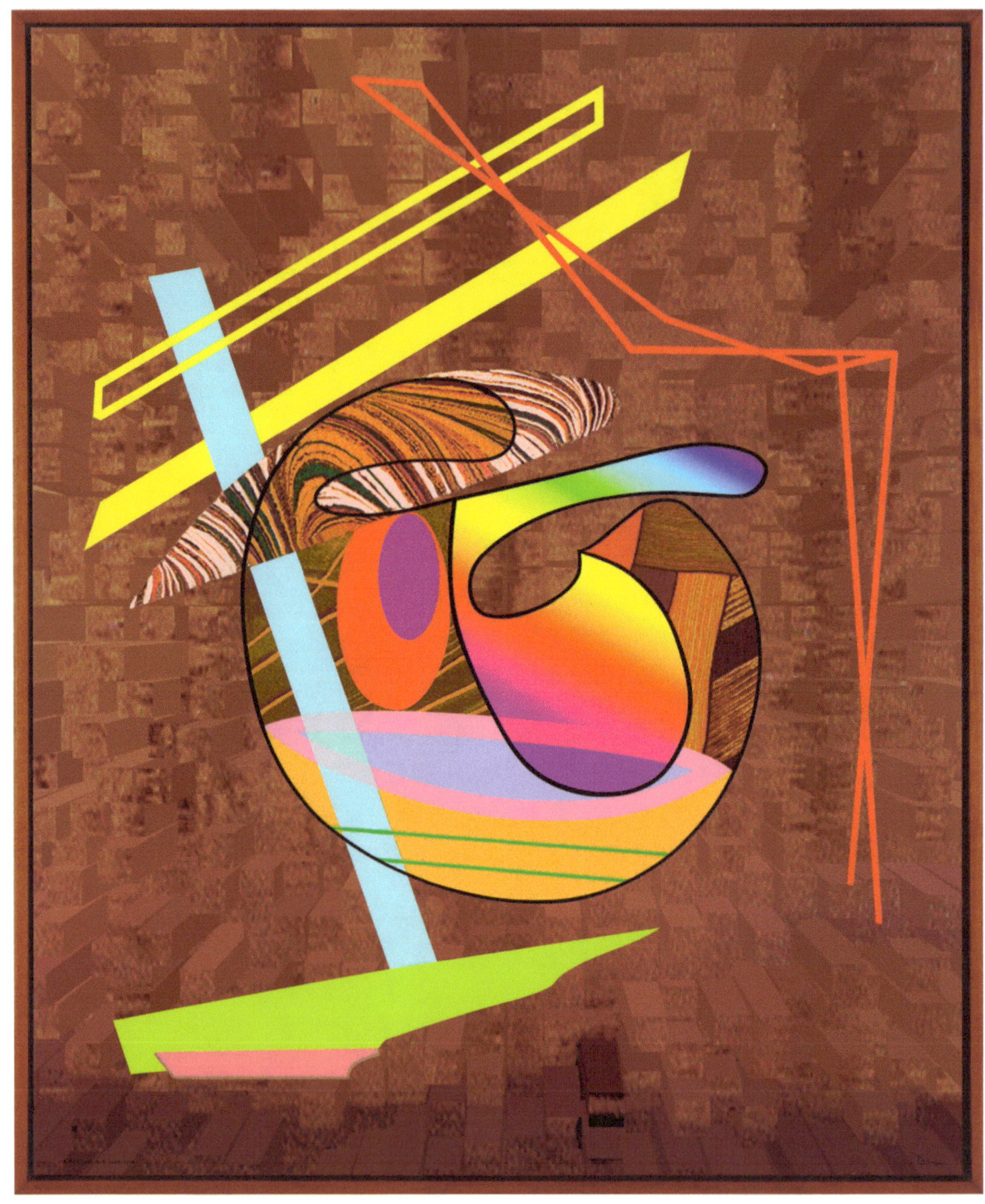

Belagio - "Headquarters" series, print on canvas, 85.7x69.2 cm (framed)

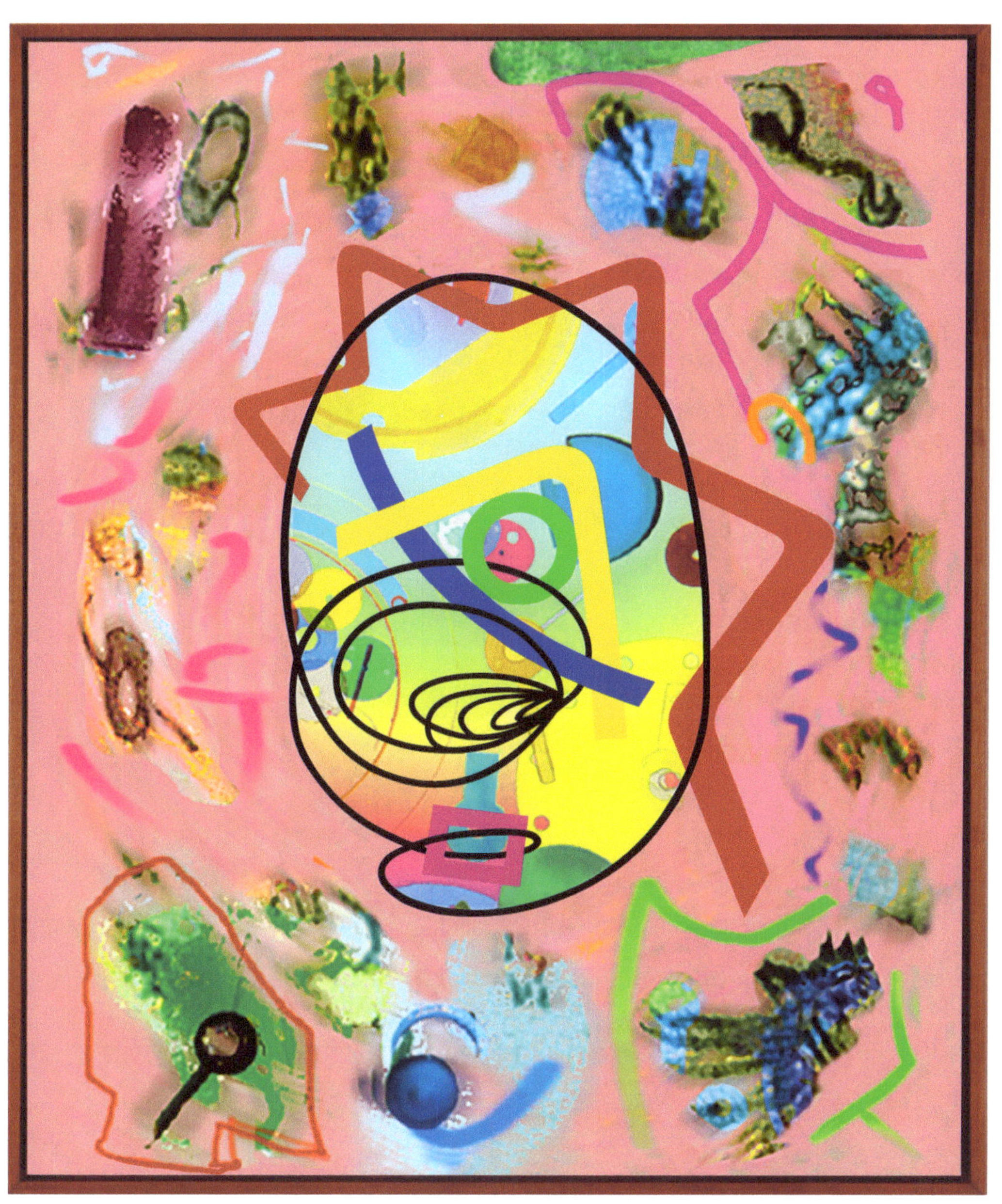

Mona - "Headquarters" series, print on canvas, 85.7x69.2 cm (framed)

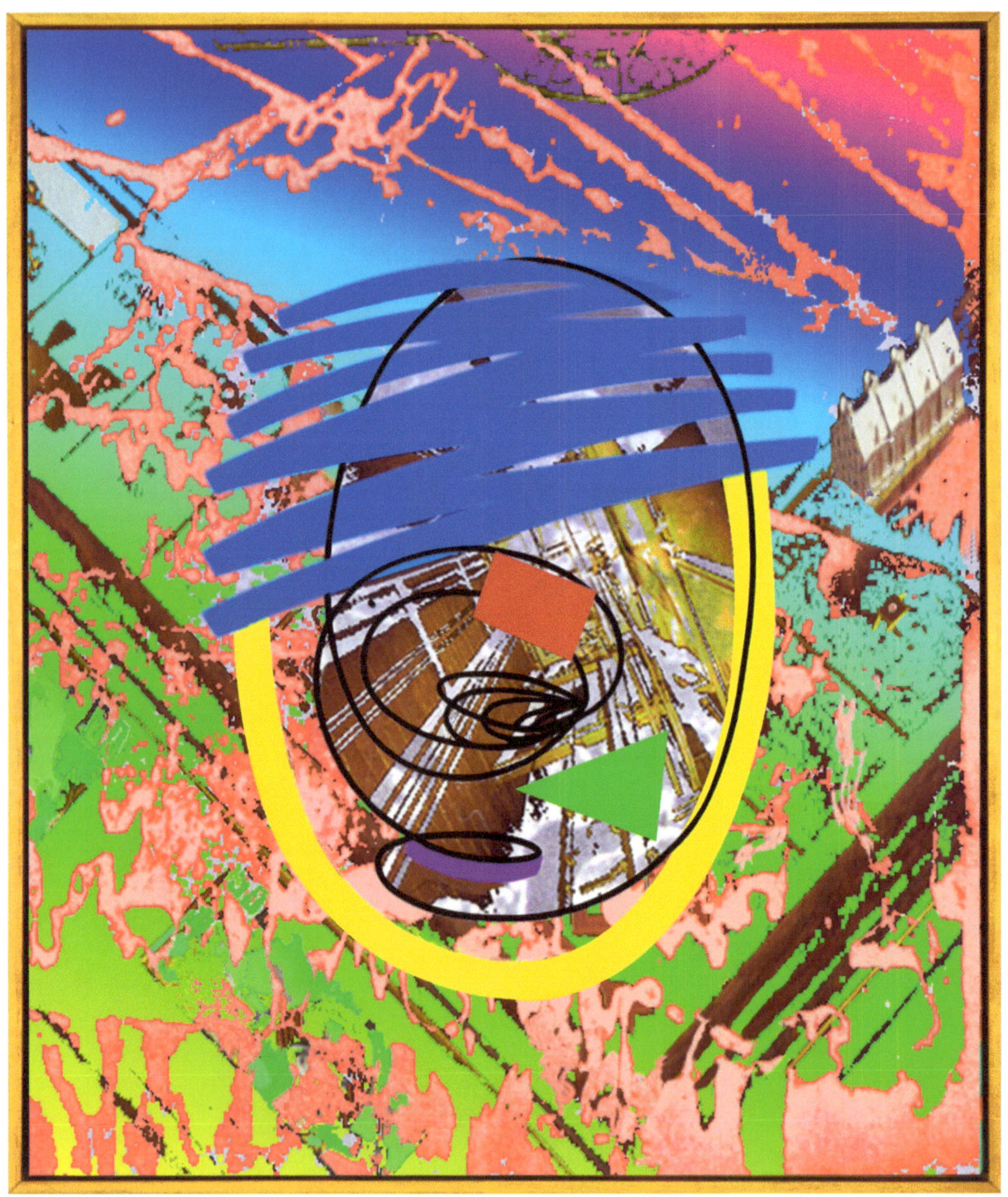

Park Place - "Headquarters" series, print on canvas, 85.7x69.2 cm (framed)

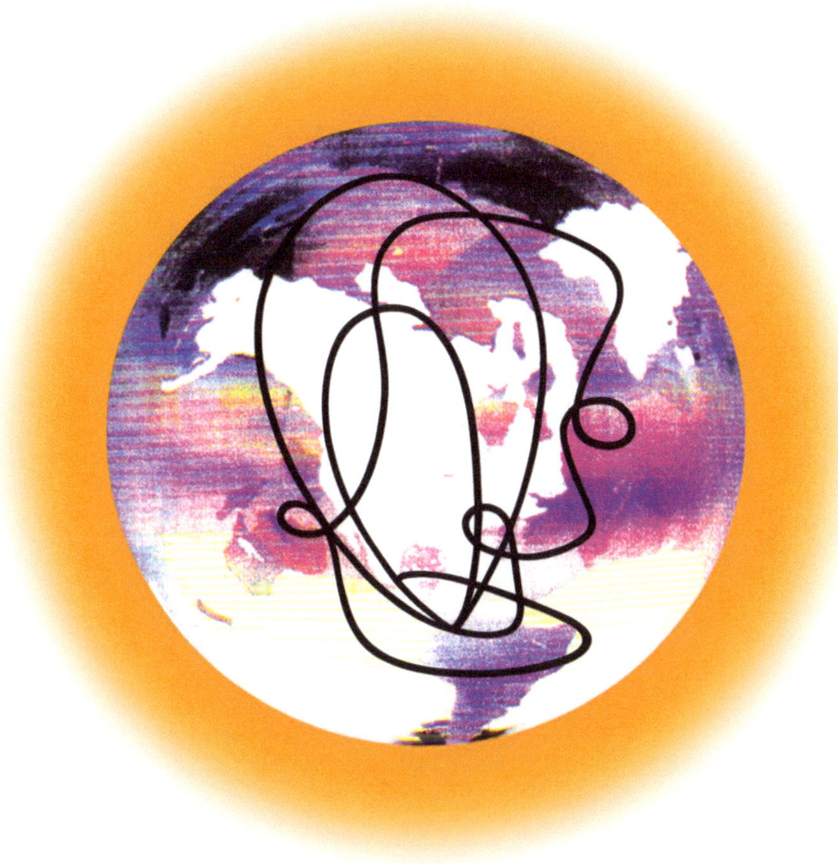

Captain Marvel - "Headquarters" series, print on paper, 64.5x54 cm (framed)

Digital Art - John Drooyan

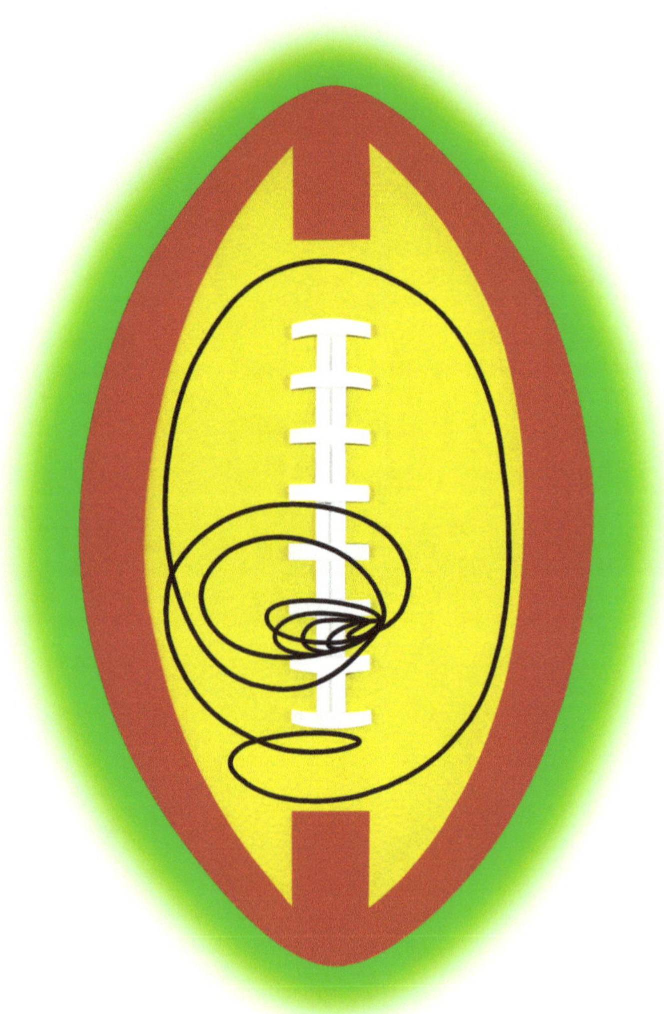

No Brainer - "Headquarters" series, print on paper, 64.5x54 cm (framed)

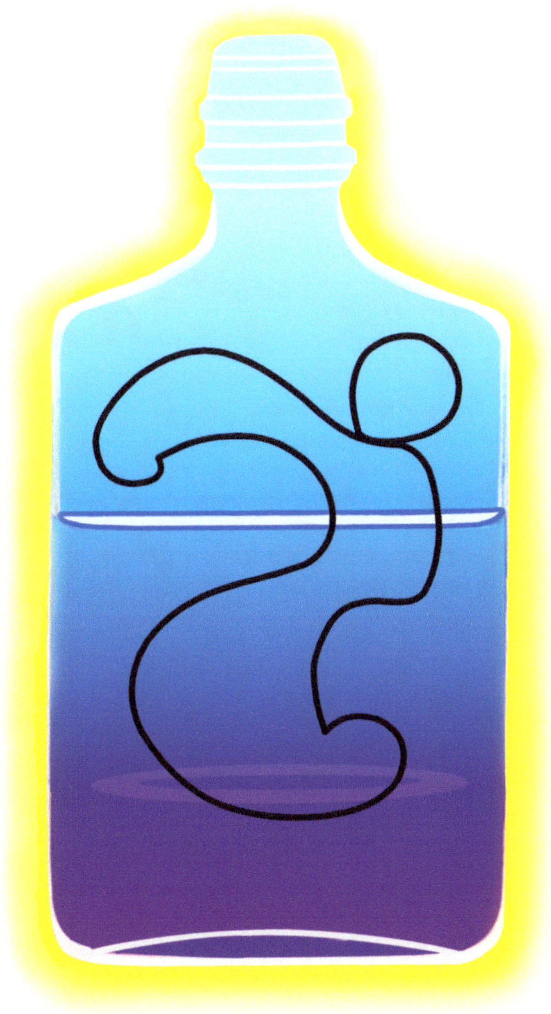

Absolute - "Headquarters" series, print on paper, 64.5x54 cm (framed)

Digital Art - John Drooyan

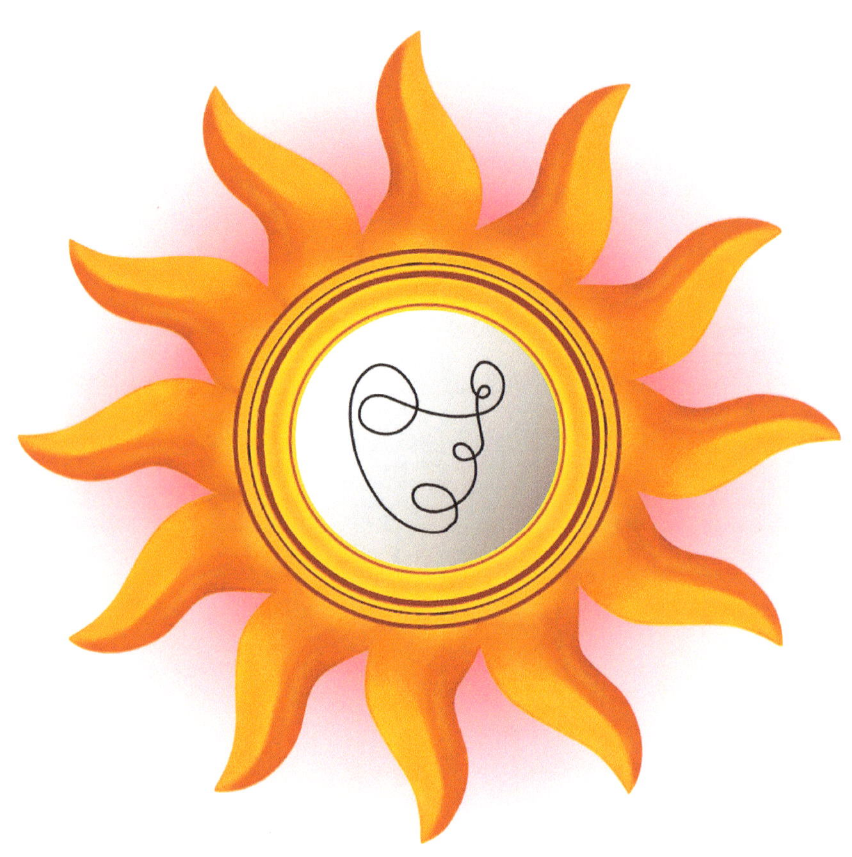

Belle De Jour - "Headquarters" series, print on paper, 64.5x54 cm (framed)

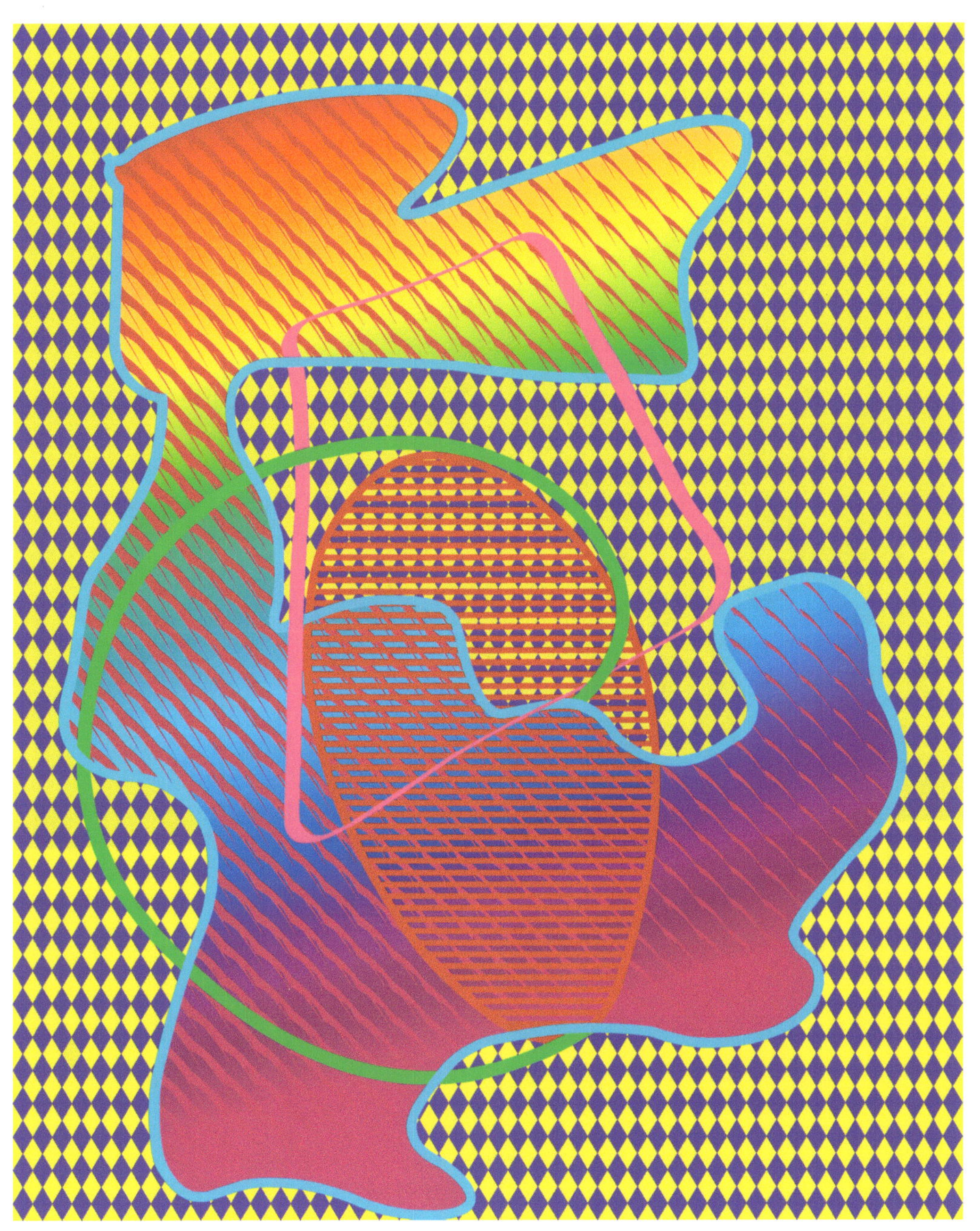

Lola - "Oceanpark" series, print on paper, 66x52 cm (unframed)

Digital Art - John Drooyan

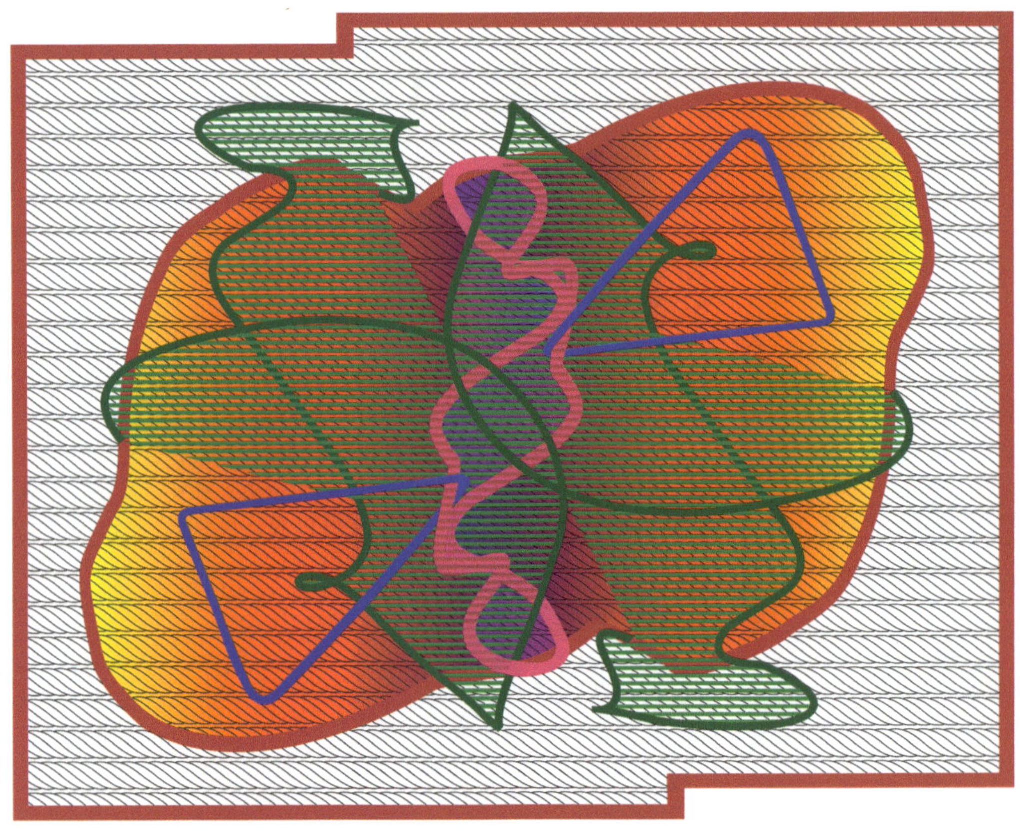

French Kiss - "Oceanpark" series, print on paper, 72x92 cm (unframed)

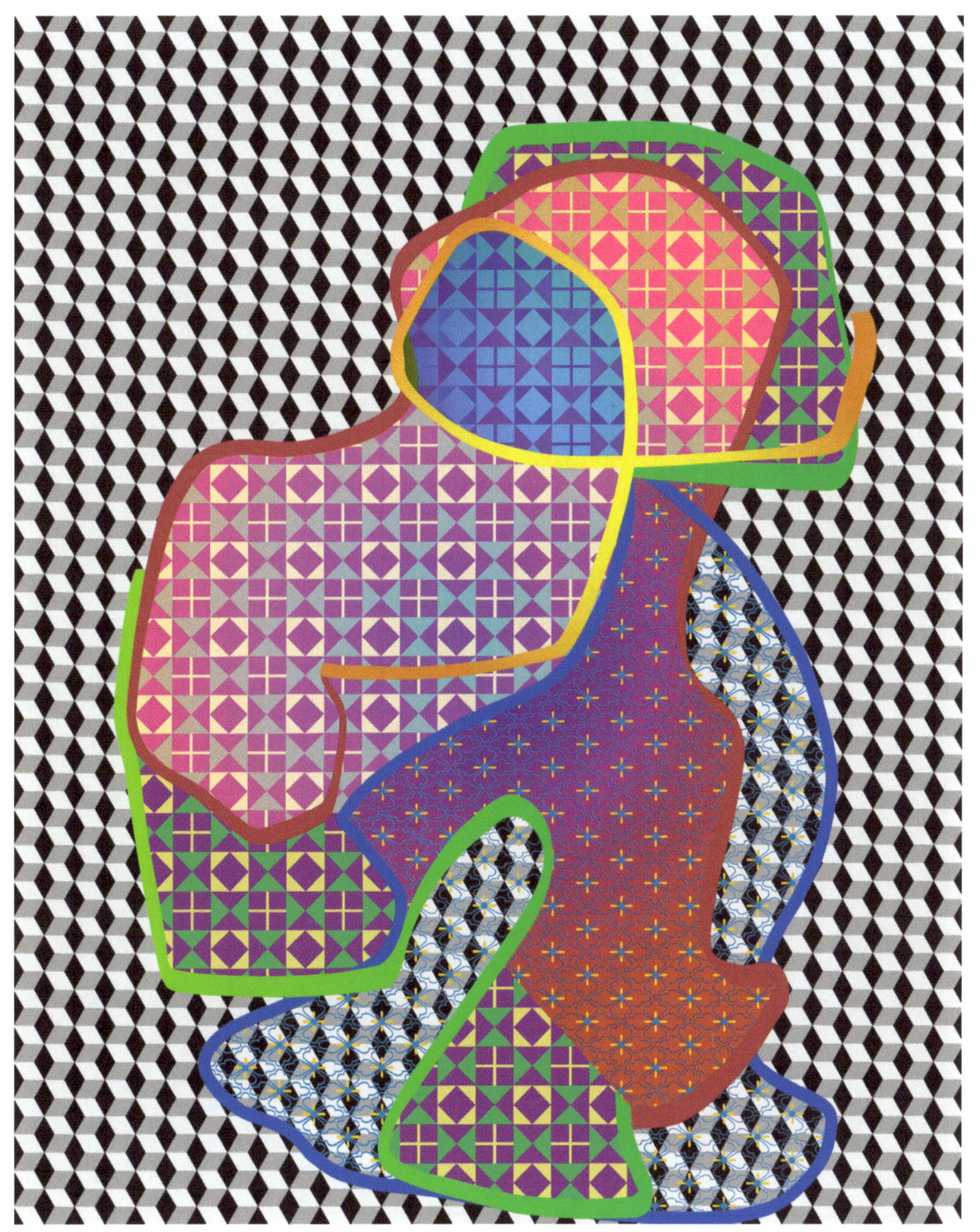

RED - "Oceanpark" series, print on paper, 66x52 cm (unframed)

Digital Art - John Drooyan

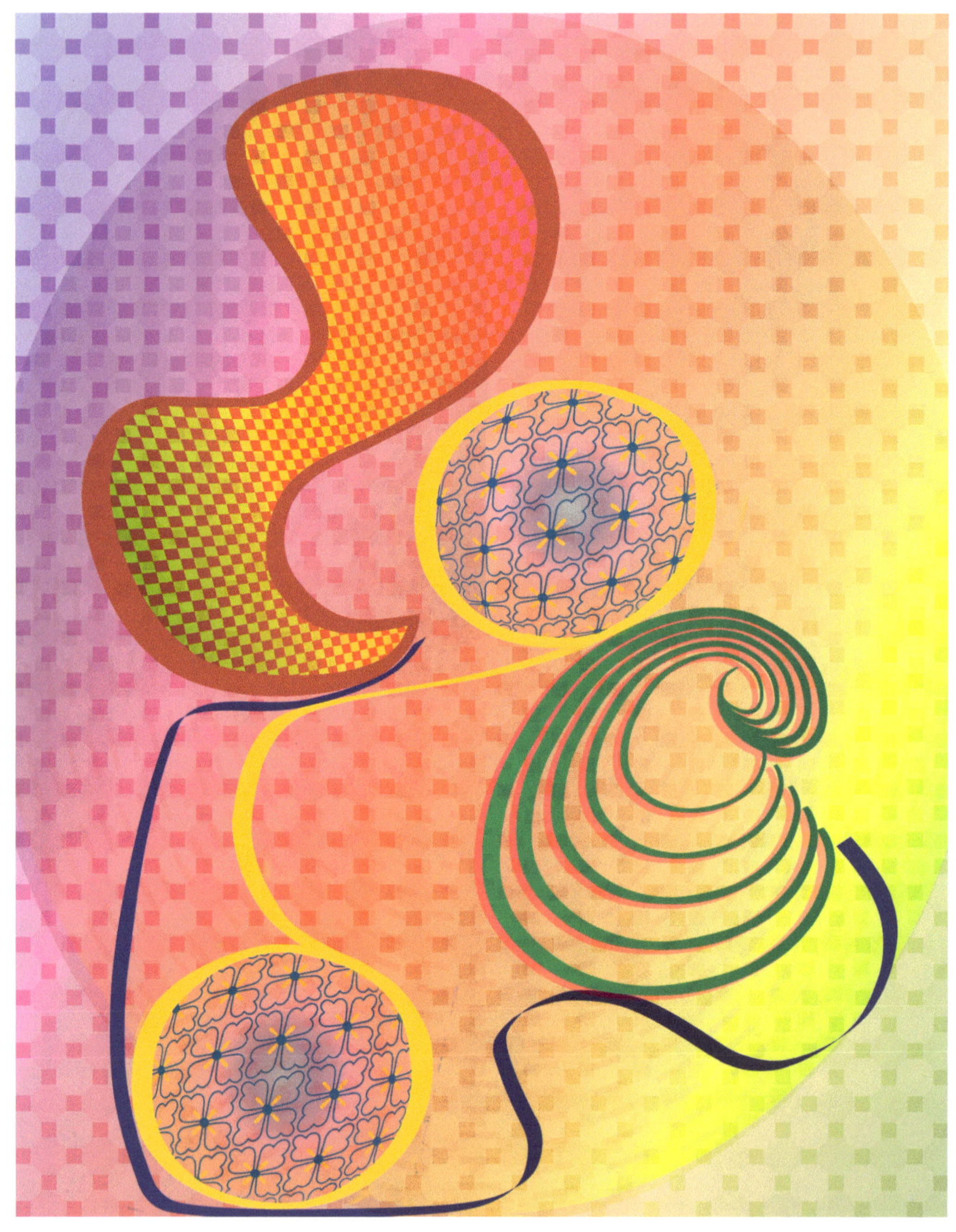

Groucho - "Oceanpark" series, print on paper, 60x47.5 cm (unframed)

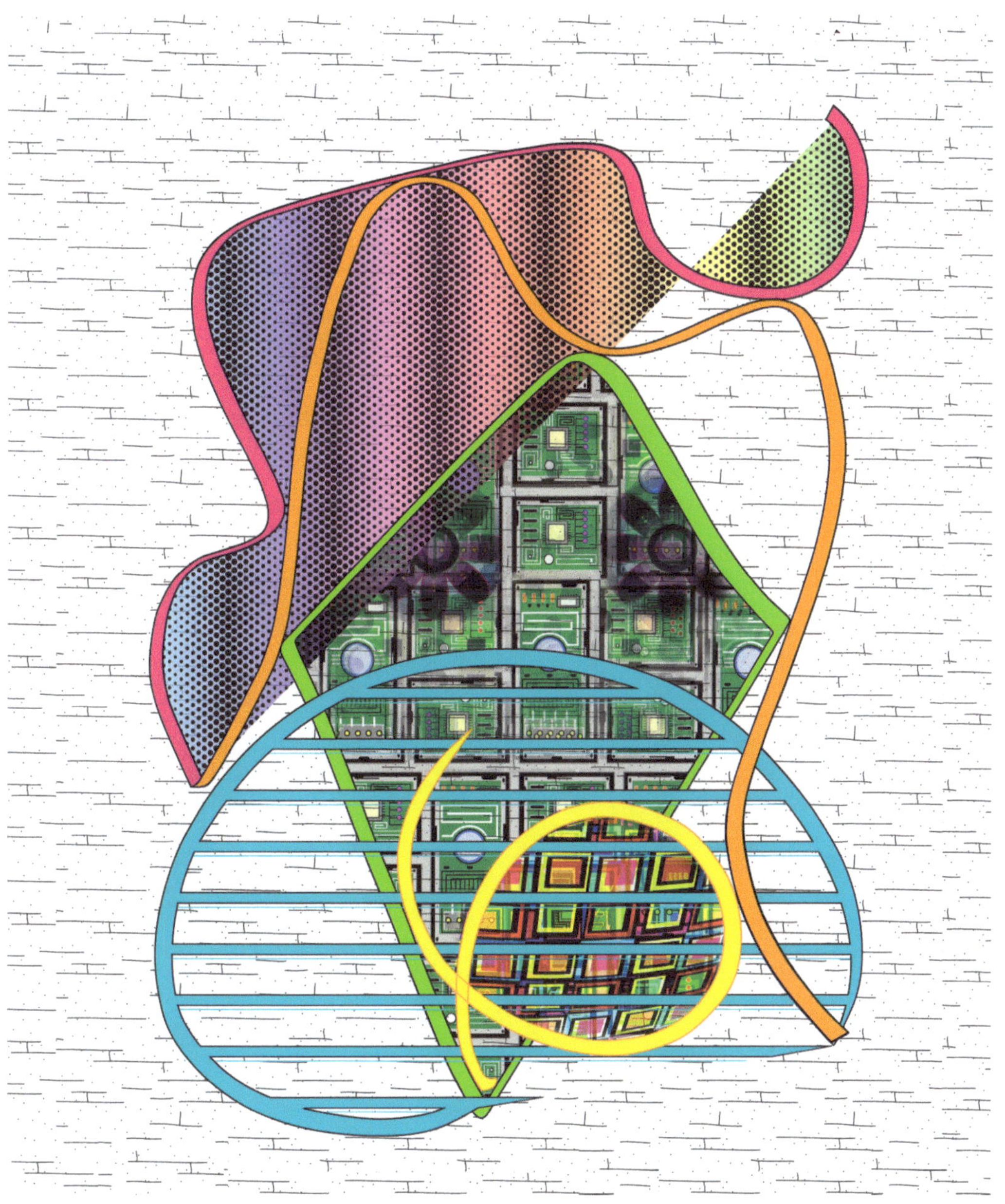

Harpo - "Oceanpark" series, print on paper, 60x47.5 cm (unframed)

Digital Art - John Drooyan

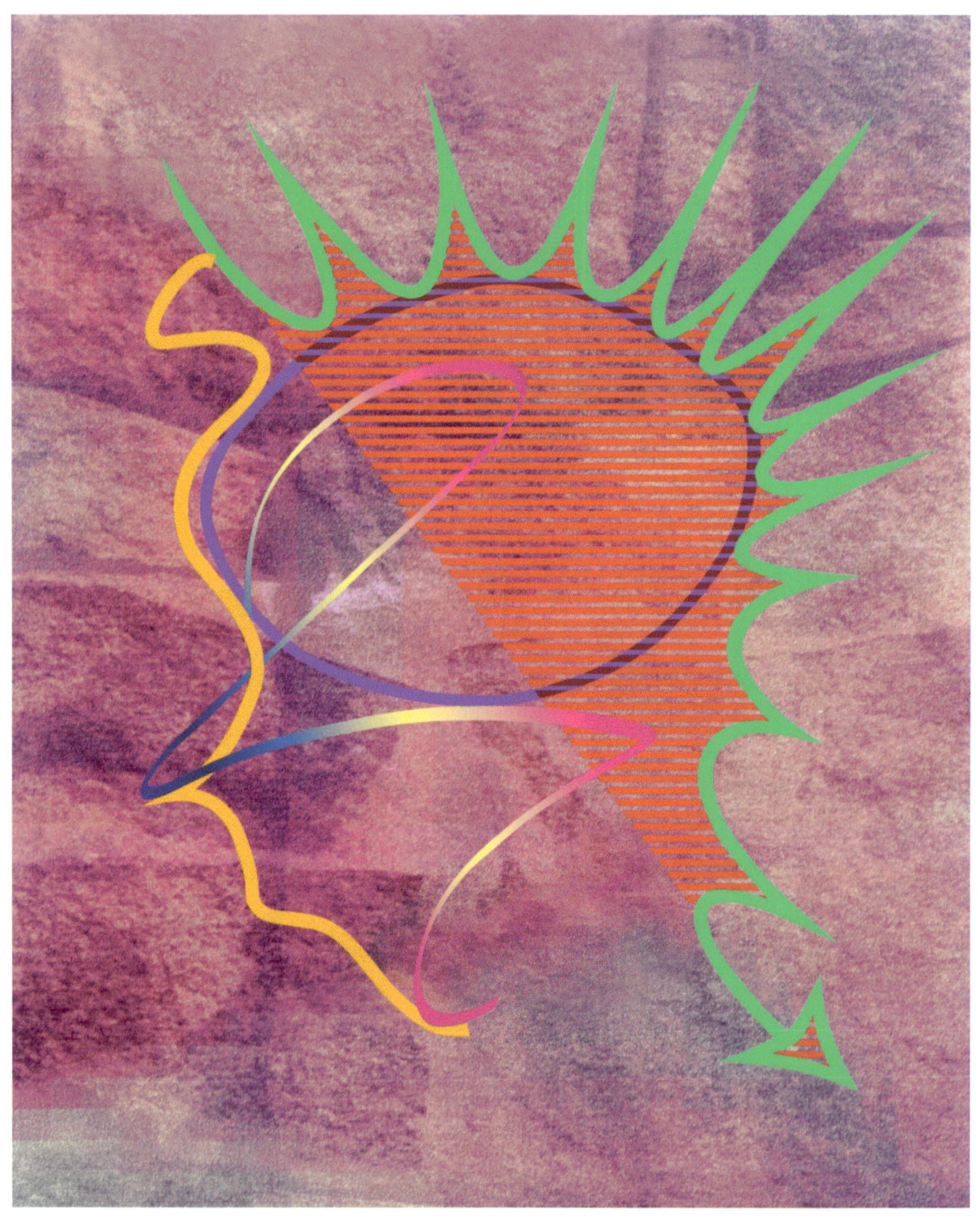

Punk - "Oceanpark" series, print on paper, 60x47.5 cm (unframed)